# PRAISE

I've just loved reading this book. Carl Reader takes a sharp pin to pop the many myths of what it takes to set up, run and scale a business. His lived experience of 'walking the walk' of setting up and running businesses burns throughout all the chapters, as does his passion for creating a business guide for the next generation.
**Sharon Davies, CEO, Young Enterprise**

Carl Reader is the guru of self-employment and this is a fantastic guide for anyone seeking to be their own boss. Whether you are looking for advice on funding, IT or building a customer base, this book has it covered.
**Elizabeth Anderson, Money and Business Editor, *i* newspaper**

It is rare to find a book that is inspiring, pragmatic, realistic and optimistic about starting out on your own and growing your own business. Carl Reader has written a business-advice book that is well-contextualized for this time, with wider learnings to support entrepreneurs. Here are practical insights into innovation, as well as aspirational business advice and worksheets to progress thinking into action. Carl explains key business knowledge and motivates the reader to move their idea forward. The Five Stars model is something I'll be using and encouraging others to!
**Siân Prime, Academic Lead (Enterprise), Goldsmiths, University of London**

Carl Reader has truly captured that the future of work is being rewritten. These Covid times will lead to the growth of the gig economy and there is a place for all skills, but we need to know how to capitalize our best skills to find our way forward. In this book, Carl has shared very useful business-centric tips and a hands-on approach to becoming a small business owner. *Boss It* will truly give you very apt learning lessons for starting your business dreams.
**Ritu Marya, Editor-in-chief, *Entrepreneur* magazine (APAC and India)**

*Boss It* is an invaluable guide to the seemingly elusive 'it' factor about self-employment. From 'dreaming it' to 'doing it', Carl Reader demystifies how to BOSS IT with confidence and clarity. This book offers the next generation an opportunity to reimagine their future working lives when it is needed now more than ever. And Carl's advice also serves as a nudge to those pondering whether to take the plunge to become their own boss. This is an important, honest and inspirational guide to make dreams a reality.

**Claire Bennison, Head, ACCA UK (Association of Chartered Certified Accountants)**

Whether you're already running your own business and need some help focusing on what's important or you're just about to embark on your first venture, you need to read this book. Carl Reader is incredibly knowledgeable about every facet of growing a robust and resilient company: every base is covered. Most importantly, for me, this isn't some romantic glamorous account of what it takes to be an entrepreneur, it's a real, gritty, practical handbook for success.

**Rebecca Burn-Callander, former Enterprise Editor, *Daily Telegraph***

Whether you're starting your first business or building your tenth, you will be more successful by applying Carl Reader's brilliant BOSS IT principles.

**Michael Heppell, *Sunday Times* bestselling author, speaker and coach**

Carl Reader is a passionate and dedicated supporter of entrepreneurs and small businesses. In this book, he takes would-be entrepreneurs through 'the good', but also doesn't shy away from 'the bad and the ugly'. Carl is an affable coach and this guide is incredibly practical, with case studies, templates and exercises, and refreshingly there's no business jargon in sight!

**Francesca James, Founder, Great British Entrepreneur Awards**

Carl Reader's #Bossit is a must-read for anyone considering starting or already running their own business. Carl's experience, insight and approachable style combine to captivate and inform far better than most business books I've read. He's honest about the realities and the

practicalities, and his approach – Dream it, Plan it, Do it, Scale it – sets it all out for you. Carl's straightforward advice demystifies complex issues and should be a constant reference source for all. Keep it handy and read it often.
**Chris Bryce, former CEO/Chair, IPSE (Association of Independent Professionals and the Self-Employed)**

*Boss It* uniquely addresses the two most important aspects of business ownership – the *why* and the *how*. Self-employment and business ownership remain the backbone of the world's economy, yet the concepts remain unimaginable or misunderstood for many. The author demystifies the topics in a way that guides the reader through self-analysis, supported by a pragmatic step-by-step process. The end result is inspiration and action for the motivated reader!
**Brad D Smith, Executive Chairman, Intuit**

Starting a business is hard. However, *Boss It* provides the recipe of success to get it right. It's what I wish I had read 30 years ago. *Boss It* gives every new founder the playbook for starting a successful business.
**Ramon Ray, Founder and Producer, Smart Hustle Media**

Purchasing this book is a no-brainer for anyone in business or thinking of doing their own thing. Carl Reader has walked the walk in his own businesses and now shares years of experience and motivation in plain English.
**Mike Michalowicz, author, *Profit First* and *Fix This Next***

# Boss It

Control your time, your income
and your life

Carl Reader

KoganPage

**Publisher's note**

Every possible effort has been made to ensure that the information contained in this book is accurate at the time of going to press, and the publisher and author cannot accept responsibility for any errors or omissions, however caused. No responsibility for loss or damage occasioned to any person acting, or refraining from action, as a result of the material in this publication can be accepted by the editor, the publisher or the author.

First published in Great Britain and the United States in 2021 by Kogan Page Limited

2nd Floor, 45 Gee Street
London
EC1V 3RS
United Kingdom

122 W 27th St, 10th Floor
New York, NY 10001
USA

4737/23 Ansari Road
Daryaganj
New Delhi 110002
India

www.koganpage.com

Kogan Page books are printed on paper from sustainable forests.

© The Startup Coach Limited, 2021

The right of The Startup Coach Limited to be identified as the author of this work has been asserted by them in accordance with the Copyright, Designs and Patents Act 1988.

**ISBNs**
Hardback    978 1 78966 643 4
Paperback   978 1 78966 641 0
eBook       978 1 78966 642 7

**British Library Cataloguing-in-Publication Data**

A CIP record for this book is available from the British Library.

**Library of Congress Cataloging-in-Publication Data**

Cataloging-in-Publication Data is available. Library of Congress Control Number: 2020034402

Typeset by Integra Software Services, Pondicherry
Print production managed by Jellyfish
Printed and bound by CPI Group (UK) Ltd, Croydon CR0 4YY

# CONTENTS

# WHO THIS BOOK IS DEDICATED TO...

Everyone who's ever written a book knows that it is like a marathon. It's painful, involves several sleepless nights and there's little fun along the way.

But for some reason, we do it again and again.

There's something special about seeing your words in print. Knowing that your knowledge can help thousands if not millions, of people.

I have one group in mind that I really want to dedicate this book to: the next generation. My kids, their classmates and everyone else in their year group. Those who are in the year above, the year below and in different schools. Across the world.

Every one of us has gone through an academic system that prioritizes an Industrial Age mindset. Get a safe job, a good 'nine to five' job, a career. Perhaps even a job for life.

That system is broken and academia hasn't caught up with it. We all crave more control but are being set up for a life of employment. Helping someone else reach their goals, under their control.

My eldest son Jordan is nearly 21 at the time of writing and didn't realize that self-employment was an option for him until recently, after years of being asked to study for exams that were irrelevant to his goals and skillsets. My youngest, Junior, is 3, and I sincerely hope that he grows up in a society that accepts self-employment and business ownership as a perfectly normal way of life.

As for Lauren, Dee and Charlie, who are all within the current system, all I can hope is that they see the example that Jordan has set for them by doing his own thing.

So this book is dedicated to the next generation – my kids, their friends and their peers.

I hope that the generation that reads this book puts the lessons into action, so that we as a society can lead by example and show our kids that there is another way. Let's make sure that we all BOSS IT.

# ABOUT THE AUTHOR

**C**arl Reader is a regular small business commentator, having appeared in most of the UK national newspapers, TV channels and radio stations. He has sat on all sides of the table – as a founder, an adviser, an entrepreneur and an investor; and retains his position of Joint Chairman at d&t. He currently serves as an ambassador to IPSE, the trade body for the self-employed in the UK and US, and as the Chair of the Practitioners Panel of the ACCA. Previously, he has served as board director of the British Franchise Association, amongst other not-for-profit and charitable efforts. Carl speaks globally to small business audiences, helping them understand that business isn't difficult. It's hard work, but it isn't difficult.

To find out more, visit www.carlreader.com

# PREFACE

At the time of writing this book, the world is going through some significant shifts. A different 'personality led' approach to politics is prevailing globally. Coronavirus is currently spreading throughout the world, with many countries on lockdown and a likely recession around the corner (see 'The world has turned on its head…', page xv). Climate change has become a climate emergency. Closer to home, the UK has just left the European Union. And in my back garden, I can see the impacts of Storm Ciara and Storm Dennis – the worst weather in the area this century.

Despite all of this stuff, I prefer to focus on what I can control.

That might sound flippant, but it is the reality of making a difference. I can't change a worldwide pandemic, but I can change my own actions and protect myself. I can't reverse an emergency, but I can be mindful of the actions I can take to help.

For me, control is a big thing. In fact, it's an essential thing.

Every time I've struggled in life, it's because of a lack of control. The realization that I need control over what I do and how I do it has been life changing. And nothing has given me more control over my day-to-day life than being my own boss.

In this book, I share the lessons that I've learned along the way – what I've learned from doing it myself and helping thousands of others.

I sincerely hope that it helps you control your time, your income and your life.

# THE WORLD HAS TURNED ON ITS HEAD...

I'm writing this in July 2020, just a few months after submitting the final manuscript to my publishers. Since writing the book, the world has turned on its head. What was referred to as a potential challenge became a very real challenge. Entire countries went into lockdown, economies plummeted and we have all been shaped by a very real and threatening public health pandemic.

## As we get back into normality, this book has never been more relevant

If you are an existing business owner, you can use the lessons within this book to help restart, rebuild and flourish (I'll come on to that in more detail in a moment).

If you have been or are currently going through the process of being furloughed, or your role being made redundant, this book can help you understand the world of business and take charge of your situation.

And if you are thinking of being your own boss, well – this book was made for you anyway!

### A note about the content within the book

One of the things that you will pick up on when reading the book is that it was written in a pre-COVID world. You will see reference to things like face-to-face networking and offices! Whilst these might seem like a distant past when you first pick this book up, rest assured that they will return in some way in the near future.

Life will be different, and the way that we assess the risks of infection will change forever, but I am still a firm believer that *business is no longer B2B or B2C, but H2H – Human to Human*. We are social beings and, whilst it might sound like a cliché, people work with people – and conversations over coffee simply cannot be replaced by keyboards and social media updates.

# How to use this book if you are an existing business owner

The position that we are in is unprecedented.

Businesses, large and small, are having to pivot. I've seen some remarkable stories first hand of how businesses have adapted over the lockdown period. Kids tuition businesses have started providing lessons online through e-learning platforms such as Thinkific and Kajabi. Clothing manufacturers have produced protective clothing for health systems. Local farm shops, butchers and bakers have started delivering food to those isolating. I even attended an online cocktail masterclass rather than visiting a bar!

Whilst these initiatives might have been necessary and sufficient to get through lockdown, the reality is that many businesses will need to build a new plan for the foreseeable future. They have taken on debt, government stimulus packages are ending and businesses globally have had to change so that they can prosper in a socially distanced world.

There are three steps to this process:

*RESTART    –    REBUILD    –    FLOURISH*

*Restart* – after any crisis like this, businesses need to hit the reset button. This is where the key learnings within the first half of this book will help take you back to the early days of business. You will learn about my 'Dream – Plan – Do – Review' process and, whilst you may not have consciously applied this process before, I would hope that this book can help you intentionally revisit your dream and your plan, so that you can design a business that works for you.

*Rebuild* – the latter part of this book is focused on scaling a business. Over the next few years, the economy will be rebuilding itself and this is entirely dependent on new and existing businesses growing simultaneously. The challenges that will face us are significant, as banks will look to strengthen their own balance sheets and will naturally become more risk averse. You will learn about the four pillars of scaling; and this can help kick off your thinking about your funding platform, your growth model, how your team is structured and how you lead the business through a new age.

*Flourish* – this bit is down to you! Allow me to help you restart and rebuild – and when your business flourishes, I sincerely hope that you enjoy the ups, having suffered the downs of the entrepreneurial rollercoaster.

# A final note for all readers

You will have seen that the subtitle of this book is 'Control your time, your income and your life'. I believe that now, more than ever before, we as individuals want to be in control of what we do and how we do it.

Whether we are employed or self-employed, we've had a taste of freedom from the nine to five. Many of us have adopted flexible working patterns around homeschooling, have cut the commute and have found a new love for athleisure rather than formal office wear.

We've also all had to use our initiative and internal motivation. We haven't had a boss looking over our shoulder, but we've cracked on and worked harder than ever. For those who have been furloughed, I've heard of inspirational stories around volunteering, mentorship and contributing to society. We've all taken control in some way over lockdown.

Now, looking forward, we have the opportunity to take control and BOSS IT.

# ACKNOWLEDGEMENTS

I would love to say this book is all my work; however, there are far too many people to mention that have come some way towards helping this book come to life.

I'd like to thank the following, in no particular order. Helen Kogan and Chris Cudmore, of Kogan Page, for taking a punt on me and trusting my experience and platform to bring this book to life. Rebecca Bush, for being a wonderfully supportive editor, going over and above my expectations and helping to shape my crazy ideas into something that is readable. My executive board at d&t, Dave Galvin and Claire Law, who help keep my business working without me, and my co-chairman Ben Herbert, for helping me through the journey from director to leader. My mastermind group – you all know who you are – for challenging me, my aspirations and my beliefs. My coach Dave Holland, who always helps me see things through a different lens, not by giving me the answers but by giving me the questions.

I'd also like to thank my colleagues across all of my business interests, my suppliers, my customers… you all help in your own way. My social media followers – yes, all 150,000 or so of you (not that I'm counting), who help drive me to continue creating content for you. I don't see myself as a thought leader, simply an opinion sharer – and it is just a happy coincidence if they happen to benefit you all. Every guest of my podcast, attendee of my keynote talks, listener of my radio interviews, social media follower and reader of my columns. You all give me a reason to keep doing what I'm doing.

And I've saved the best to last – my wonderful wife Sarah. Her tolerance, love, understanding and support has helped me get to the position so that I can write this book, has helped me get on with writing this book and helps me every day to fulfil my mission of helping others. Thank you, Wifey x

# Introduction

## Be your own boss

The world is becoming self-employed at a rapid rate. We've all heard of the 'gig economy' and freelancing. In my home country, the UK, one in seven of us are now self-employed.[1] More businesses are being set up now than ever before. But for many, the idea of taking control and being their own boss seems out of reach.

But what is it that makes this goal seem so unreachable? In my recent Twitter poll of approximately 300 Twitter respondents, the joint leaders were: a lack of money and a lack of confidence.

The results of this poll were what motivated me to write this book. I knew at that point that I had the chance to provide common-sense advice in plain English to help those who feel trapped in employment, earning income for their boss's businesses.

It all comes back to confidence.

We can easily blame our own personal limiting factors on external circumstances – and maybe that is the case, but I'd be willing to bet that external factors are less limiting for most people than we think. We can always moan about not having endless piles of cash or being worked to the bone in the day job – and again, those things are probably true, but they're not necessarily the barrier you think they are. For most people, we could always find just enough time and cash to get started, if we really wanted to – so often, it's not the lack of money or time that really gets in people's way; it's self-doubt and fear.

You see, I would argue that being your own boss is fairly easy. Despite the (often well-meaning) advice that can cause us to think twice, I firmly believe that there are just a few simple principles that you need to adhere to, and a few psychological barriers that you need to overcome, in order to be successful in business.

These principles aren't complicated and they can easily be applied to any business. They are based on the thousands of businesses that I've helped, and I've learned how to refine them for my keynote talks, my advice columns and my podcasts. Very simply, the principles in this book allow you to identify what you need to do to start or grow a business.

There is also a lot of confusion out there. Even the words that we use to describe business owners evoke different feelings and reactions. We often hear anything from self-employed to entrepreneur, with phrases such as mumpreneur, network marketer, freelancer, partner, investor, company owner, and many more thrown into the mix. Each has its own connotations; however, there are never enough words to describe the individual make-up and motivations of everyone looking to do their own thing. Everybody is unique, and every business is unique. This book aims to help you embrace that uniqueness, and find the magic within you and your business.

I would just have one last word of warning to anyone looking to invest in themselves before going it alone.

There are far too many sharks out there who are simply out to make a quick buck. If you've done any research before picking up this book, I'm sure you would have come across 'guaranteed' ways to make millions online, and 'unbelievable' processes to transform your life. Back in the early 2000s, the internet was awash with Google Adsense schemes that could set you up for financial freedom. Since then, we've seen affiliate marketing schemes, e-learning courses about 'funnels' and automation, membership groups and many other similar products. Internet marketing to potential future internet marketers is perhaps the world's biggest pyramid scheme, and for every self-professed guru there seem to be a thousand willing punters who hope that a $97 course will transform their life.

I hate to break it to you, but the reality is really nothing like that, and I can't promise you that you will get rich quick.

However, what I *can* do is offer you the chance to live your own life, on your own terms, and with the control of your destiny that is only available by being your own boss. What's more, the business that you will build will be sustainable, on strong foundations, and not reliant on the latest marketing fads.

Being in business is a journey. Or sometimes, a rollercoaster ride. There are tremendous highs and tortuous lows. You will find that there are some days where you can't believe your luck, and others where you want to hide and hope for the best. I can pretty much guarantee one thing, though: once you've had a taste for it, you won't go back to being employed.

Welcome to the world of the unemployable!

## A note on language

You wouldn't have picked this book up without some level of curiosity about the strange world that business owners seem to live in. We all have our own slant on it: maybe we think that business owners must be entrepreneurs like Bill Gates, turning everything that they touch into gold. Or, on the other end of the scale, maybe we had a family member who ran a struggling business, working every waking hour just to put food on the table. Whatever your ideas about business owners might have been before picking up this book, you're probably right to a certain extent: the reality of running a business actually encompasses both of these extremes, and many more in between the two of them. There is no normal when it comes to the world of business ownership, and the language this book uses reflects that.

Some people like to describe themselves as entrepreneurs; others like to say that they are 'in business', but throughout this book, different phrases will be used at different times, with no negative or positive connotations attached to each. In my eyes, a business owner is an entrepreneur, and vice versa. There is, however, a big difference between a business owner and a self-employed individual, which we will come on to later in the book.

# Part One
# Dream it

# 01
# Why should you be your own boss?

In this chapter you will:

- find out the realities of running a business;
- understand why people start, and stay, in business;
- find out about the difference between a business and self-employment;
- find out about the different types of business owner.

**B**efore you even start thinking about whether you *should* be your own boss, you need to consider why you would *want* to be your own boss. What is it that made you pick up this book? Is it the culmination of a lifelong dream, or a moment inspired by a motivational quote on social media? Are you thinking about a bigger vision that you have, or just trying to escape the rat race of employment? We all have different triggers, and understanding what has driven us to this point can prove extremely helpful when things don't go to plan.

I hate to put a dampener on things, particularly this early in the book, but there are a few realities of running a business which don't tend to get shared publicly. I didn't promise this journey would be easy! Let's just mull over these first.

# The realities of running a business

## Reality check 1: You won't escape the rat race

I hate to say it, but it's true. Often, when we are stuck in a mundane day job, we can look at business owners with some level of envy. Perhaps it's the flexible schedules, the lack of a boss, or a preconceived idea of the pots of money that most business owners are sat on.

These thoughts might make great daydreams, but the reality is that almost all self-employed individuals end up in a rat race of their own, and many business owners do too (we'll cover the differences between the two later, as this will be a recurring theme during the book). Before diving into a new venture blindly, it's important to understand that business is hard work, and in the early days there's likely to be little financial reward.

One of the harsh realities of starting a business is that there is no such thing as a 'market rate' for your time as a business owner. Nor is there even the concept of a 'minimum wage'. You might look at self-employed plumbers charging £80 per hour, but the reality is that they have to spend many unbilled hours marketing their business, travelling between jobs, doing their admin, or simply waiting for more work to come in. In the early days, you have to expect that there will be an investment of both money and unpaid work to build a business.

## Reality check 2: Things won't go to plan

Again, this is another sign that it's not easy. I'd love to say that I've seen a business hit its projections perfectly, but it never happens. In fact, I can almost certainly say that you won't hit your financial and operational projections exactly. In all likelihood, you'll have more chance of winning the lottery than getting every figure and ratio exactly right before you've started. There are too many unknowns in the future; trying to be penny-perfect in your projections is unrealistic.

In my experience, that means that you will be more likely to be optimistic in your plans rather than pessimistic. You are more likely to predict that you will have more customers, with a higher average spend, and better profit margins. And you are more likely to forget some of the costs of your business in your forecasts. I haven't run a statistical analysis on all of the businesses I have advised to verify this fact – but I also can't remember a single business that has massively outperformed its wildest expectations.

There's a simple reason for this. When any of us look at a new venture, we look at it optimistically; if we weren't being optimistic, we probably wouldn't do it! Think about it logically – why would you leave a stable, secure job to do something that won't work? Leaving behind the comfort of a guaranteed monthly income, surrounded by work colleagues and the luxury of weekends is a tough step, and most of us wouldn't ditch it without dreaming of something far better.

All that said, optimism isn't a reason to not go ahead with building a business. Far from it. In fact, you need to embrace any optimism that you have, as you will need it during the highs and lows of starting and growing a business. It is also a vital asset during your vision-setting and in the early days of running the business. Just make sure that you keep your optimism in check when preparing your projections and plans for the business.

## Reality check 3: You will be tested beyond your comfort zone

Being your own boss seems easy. You can choose when you want to come into work, park right next to the door and have assistants to do everything from your typing through to organizing your next corporate entertaining trip. And your employees will do the 'real' work as well, won't they?!

These thoughts are commonplace in those with an employee mindset. But the reality of doing your own thing is actually very different. In the early days you will be everything, doing every single job. You'll be the managing director, the typist and the coffee server. You'll most probably be the cleaner as well! You will be doing things that you don't want to do, and things that you don't know how to do.

Very early on in the business journey, you'll have a realization of exactly how much you don't know. And it's almost certainly quite a lot! While you might have experience in some of the vital areas – such as sales perhaps, or finance – you will soon find that the reality of juggling your sales skills with the analytical detail needed from a finance director, while also managing an outsourced team of developers and searching for suitable suppliers, is a tough ask.

You will also find that the emotional rollercoaster will be far more thrilling than anything that you would have encountered in employment. If the cash flow projections for the month look a little tight, it's not someone else's problem – it's yours. In the early days, you will own every single win and loss in the business, and the emotion around each will be magnified. There will be times that will be stressful beyond imagination, and other times where you couldn't imagine life being any different. Dealing with these ups and downs in business is one of the main strengths in most business owners that continue beyond the first couple of years.

## Reality check 4: You will work longer, and harder, than you ever did for a boss

There is a great phrase that I think sums up most self-employed people:

*You go from working for a jerk to working for a maniac.*

Those of you who have already made the leap into self-employment are probably reading the above with a wry smile. The stresses of not hitting your initial targets, and learning on the job, often force you to work extremely unsociable hours in order to get by. I once heard that the best thing about being self-employed is that you can choose exactly which 18 hours per day you want to work.

As your business grows, you will probably find that your level of input grows as well, until you reach the point at which you have a truly scalable business with a management and leadership team. The reality, however, is that only a very small percentage of businesses ever reach the size needed to afford a team capable of releasing the business owner from the day-to-day grind. In fact, only 4 per cent of UK businesses ever reach £1 million turnover, and of those, only 10 per cent ever reach £10 million turnover.[1] Even in businesses turning over £10 million per year, I still find business owners slaving away as an integral part of the team.

There *are* ways to scale effectively and build a business that is not reliant on you: I wouldn't have had the time and freedom to write this book if that wasn't the case. But there are many sacrifices, not least financial, that need to be made to achieve that. In the last section of this book, we'll look at how to build a truly scalable business, if that's what you're after.

## Reality check 5: You and your business will become intertwined

That's right. You know those weird folk who are always checking emails and making business calls while on holiday? They usually aren't doing it for someone else.

A strange thing happens when you run your own business: you find that your personal world and your work world are no longer separate. Business acquaintances become personal friends, and vice versa. Weekends become weekdays, and weekdays become weekends. Work–life balance often becomes a lot harder to achieve; work and life may even slowly become one and the same.

That's not to say that you shouldn't have downtime from the business. In fact, that couldn't be further from the truth. Every business owner needs to take time out to recharge their batteries, and to reassess what they are doing and why they are doing it. Certainly in the early days of running a business, though, you will find that separation between your personal and business life becomes harder and harder.

If you're going into business, you need to come to terms with the fact that you'll never again clock off at 5pm on a Friday.

---

### A moment to reflect

Do these reality checks put you off? If not, think next about the impact that running a business might have on your family, or other dependants. It's important not to be deluded about the realities of building a business.

---

# So why *should* you be your own boss?

If you're still with me, you've shown the first sign of resilience that a business owner needs! You may also be wondering why on earth you would want to start a business, if I've just painted such a negative picture. Well, I genuinely believe that while the realities listed above might hold true for us all, there *is* some kind of magic that comes from them. This magic happens when you are in control of your own destiny: you don't see it, but it's certainly there. Despite all the work, and hardship, and struggle, you still feel energized and fulfilled. Why? Because you are on the first steps towards what is known as self-actualization.

For those who haven't undertaken formal management training, please allow me to briefly explain. There is a model by a gentleman named Abraham Maslow, in which he sets out the five tiers of human motivation.[2] This model starts with our basic human needs of food and shelter (the physiological needs), and moves through safety, belonging and esteem until we reach the final tier of self-actualization. In fact, the best definition of self-actualization came from Maslow himself, who defined it as a desire 'to become everything one is capable of becoming'.[3]

## Why do we actually do it?

This magic might explain why people continue in what might seem an illogical journey of hard work with little reward, but it doesn't explain why so many of us want to start the journey in the first place. In fact, in a survey by World Options, 68 per cent of respondents either wanted to start their own business or were actively making steps towards it.[4] Deep down, most of us know that the facade of entrepreneurship that is glamourized on TV and on social media is not as it seems, and we have at least some level of appreciation of the five realities listed above. So why do people actually start businesses?

It would be tempting for me to guess the reasons. After all, I've done it myself, and I know my own motivations! Instead of simply transferring my own beliefs and ideas onto others, though, let's look at some of the research already out there.

In 2015 a software company, Keap, alongside Audience Audit Inc., surveyed nearly 800 small businesses[5] (with 25 or fewer employees) in the United States, to gain a deeper understanding of their attitudes at both the start of their business and at the point of survey. They created four distinct profiles of respondent, and the surveyed businesses fell into the profiles almost equally:

- **Passionate Creators** (25 per cent): The Passionate Creators started their business out of love for what they do and believe wholeheartedly that passion is a crucial quality of successful small business owners. Their stated goals are often 'doing the work I love', and often refer to themselves as 'entrepreneurs' rather than any other term. The survey results also identify the Passionate Creators as the most successful and optimistic profile.

- **Freedom Seekers** (23 per cent) – The Freedom Seekers started their businesses because they value the ability to control their work experience. They want to be in charge of their schedule, career path and work environment. The respondents typically have built their businesses around flexibility and are the least likely of the four profiles to have more than one other employee.

- **Legacy Builders** (28 per cent) – The Legacy Builders believe that small businesses are more ethical and vital to the economy compared with larger corporations. They started their business to bring something new to the marketplace. It provides them with a sense of stability for their future and the future of their family, and they have created a business to help secure their retirement.

- **Struggling Survivor** (24 per cent) – The Struggling Survivor profile represents the cold, hard truth of business ownership: sometimes running a small business is scarier than it is rewarding. The majority of this category are self-employed with no employees, they are the least optimistic about entrepreneurship, and it is likely that the reason that they went into business is a long-forgotten dream.

As you can see from the above, there is a wide range of reasons why people decide to do their own thing. Some want to escape a job, some have no option, and others have an itch that they need to scratch. Everybody comes into self-employment with their own motivations and dreams.

---

### A moment to reflect

Why are *you* doing this? Without a strong reason behind you, you will find it very difficult to stay motivated.

The above reasons have come from experienced business owners who are reflecting on the reasons why they made the jump in the first place. If you are asked the same question in five years' time, how will you answer?

---

## What is the difference between self-employment and a business?

I've mentioned already that there is a difference between self-employment and owning a business. This is perhaps the biggest confusion within the business community, and once you see the difference you will find yourself frustrated with those that deliberately confuse the two.

Perhaps the easiest way to differentiate between self-employment and a business is to consider whether the business could proceed without the owner being involved in the business every day. This is a really quick way of identifying whether a business is scalable: simply put, if the business has the potential to fundamentally keep going without the day-to-day involvement of the owner, it is a business, and a scalable one at that. If the owner is an integral part of the purpose and day-to-day running, and the business would fail without them, then that person is self-employed.

It's worth bearing in mind, too, that not everybody wants to start a scalable business. In fact, most businesses are indeed run and operated by self-employed individuals. Of the 5.5 million businesses in the UK, 76 per cent have no employees. Furthermore, 94 per cent of these businesses with no employees operate from a single site, such as a home office or that of a contractor.[6] In other words, it is completely possible to 'be your own boss' while not actually being a boss at all, and working instead for a corporate contractor.

Of course, it's not a binary thing. The phases of self-employment, business owner and entrepreneur cover several different working arrangements and a number of different types of businesses, and could theoretically apply to an Uber driver as much as they could apply to individuals like Richard Branson. It's clear that there are huge differences between these two examples, and as such it is probably inappropriate to confuse their business models.

So, we've touched on a simple way of differentiating between self-employed individuals and businesses: we can take this differentiation one step further by identifying the sources of income in each business. A self-employed individual is reliant on their own endeavours and the hours that they put into the business, as these have a direct correlation to their personal income. On the other hand, a business generates income from the efforts of a number of employees and revenue from a number of customers. So, using this model, we can say that a self-employed individual is reliant on one source of income, whereas a business owner is reliant on multiple sources of income, even if they are all received within one legal entity.

There is no right or wrong answer to the question of whether you should be self-employed or look to build a business. All of us have different skillsets, different experiences, and as we'll see below, different personalities that could impact the way that we look to build and grow a business.

What does this mean to someone considering whether they want to be their own boss?

It is important for any prospective business owner to truly understand what it is that they want their business to be. Many self-employed individuals are happy with being self-employed and have no wish to build scalable businesses. It might be that they enjoy doing what they do, and they're content with simply cutting out a boss telling them how to do it. On the other hand, they might enjoy the increased income that they receive by invoicing their customers directly. A self-employed business is just as important to both the business owner and the economy as a much larger business. However, if you set out to build a scalable business, you may become frustrated if you have to operate as a sole trader due to constraints such as funding. Similarly, if you wish to be self-employed, you may find that managing multiple employees stretches you beyond your comfort zones and desires, and in turn you won't find the business as satisfying as it could be.

# How can you choose what type of business to run?

In his book *The E-Myth Revisited*, Michael Gerber describes the entrepreneur, the manager and the technician:[7]

- **the entrepreneur** – the visionary who finds it easy to set big picture plans, but finds that they get bogged down in the detail;

- **the manager** – thrives on systems and processes, and likes to make sure everything is structured and organized;
- **the technician** – likes to do a job, and to do a job well, without too much interference from a manager or an entrepreneur.

This description of the three types of personalities can be looked at as a more user-friendly version of the business model which categorizes employees as the strategic, tactical and operational sides of any business. To summarize: the **operational** functions of any business focus on routine, the simple day-to-day matters; whereas the **tactical** part of a business (the management layer) focuses on medium-term decisions and the implementation of the **strategy**, decided by the strategists (or, the entrepreneur).

Bringing this theory from management jargon back into plain English, any prospective business owner needs to decide where they sit between these personality types, and how they would like their business to develop. If you are naturally a technician, and enjoy the work that you do, you may find management uncomfortable. Likewise, if you are naturally a manager, you might find it easier to work with a team where you can add true value.

Please note that we're not making any kind of value judgement between the three personality types here; each is as valid as the next, and there are no limitations to your business regardless of your personality type. In fact, some of the fastest growing start-ups in recent times have been founded by technicians, rather than stereotypical entrepreneurs. The important thing is to understand what type of personality you have, and to make sure that your business is built in such a way that you are comfortable with starting and growing it.

And, of course: this analysis of personalities is rather simplistic, and most people are made up of elements of all three personality types. Bearing all of those caveats in mind, though, this model can serve as a useful way of appraising yourself, and it will help you understand how your business needs to look in the future.

## A moment to reflect

What kind of business owner are you? Entrepreneur, manager, or technician? If you find it hard to decide, try thinking about your co-workers and managers, and put them into the various categories. Think about how they approach things, and whether they fit the mould in which they are employed. This might help you understand what to look for when appraising yourself – which is always tougher to do!

## Chapter 1 summary

In this chapter we have looked at the reality of starting a business. We have seen that it isn't anywhere near as glamorous as it is sometimes made out to be. If you are still reading at the end of this chapter, you've got some of the resilience needed to make it in business!

Before proceeding to the next chapter, you should:

1  Think about all of the reflective questions within the chapter.

2  Download and review the Chapter 1 supplementary material from www.carlreader.com/bossit

3  Answer these questions:

o  What kind of business do I want?
   – *Self-employed / Business*

o  What kind of personality do I have?
   – *Technician / Manager / Entrepreneur*

o  Why am I starting a business?

   _____
   _____
   _____
   _____

# 02
# The difference between success and failure

In this chapter you will:

- find out the differences between employment and being your own boss;
- understand the four key elements to running a successful business;
- find out where most businesses fall down, and what causes their failure;
- understand more about what it takes to be a successful business owner.

In the last chapter, we made a deliberately negative start. Well done for making it through! This will be a common theme throughout your business journey. Business isn't easy: it may be simple, but it's not easy. If it was, everyone would be doing it and living their own dream.

# A successful business owner: there's no such thing as the typical entrepreneur

Of course, everyone is not their own boss. Everyone can't be… but I hope what was clear from the last chapter is that *anyone can be*. The popular stereotype is that every entrepreneur is a young, dynamic individual who wouldn't look out of place on *The Apprentice*. The reality is that business owners come in all shapes and sizes, and simply cannot be classified by sex, age, race or upbringing. While you might see stories in the newspapers about teen whizz-kids who build multi-million-pound apps, what you don't hear about is the legions of elder workers who start their own business just a few years away from the state retirement age. You might hear about entrepreneurs being kick-started by family money, but you don't hear about all the entrepreneurs across the world who start after bankruptcy, with no money whatsoever. The point is this: there are no limitations when it comes to who can start a business.

In fact, you could be living next door to an entrepreneur, and not even realize.

> ## A moment to reflect
>
> What's stopping you from starting a business? Do you hold any beliefs about what an entrepreneur 'needs to be' – age, financial background, race, neurodiversity – that might be acting as barriers to your goal?

By now, you already know the differences between being self-employed and owning a scalable business, and you also understand the different personality types in business. Regardless of your own personality type and intentions, there are some very real differences between employment and being your own boss which you need to be aware of.

## Room to fail

I mentioned in the introduction that one of the two leading factors stopping people from starting their own business, based on my survey, is confidence. Many simply don't have the confidence that their business will be a success; that they will attract enough customers to pay the bills; and most importantly for some, they don't have the confidence that they won't fail.

This opens up the crux of the difference between employment and self-employment. In employment, it's rare that you are allowed to fail. Here in the UK, employment rights stop companies firing staff at will, and as such there is a comfort blanket for each of us. If we don't quite perform, we can be put on 'performance management' and coached to help improve our performance. And if that doesn't work out, there's always a sideways step into another role, or the opportunity to jump before you are pushed. And where there is at-will employment, the point stands – employee turnover is expensive in both time and money for employers, and so many bosses and businesses are reluctant to let people go quickly. Even without the law, as an employee, that safety blanket is still there to a certain extent.

In business, the market is a crueller judge. The market decides whether you are performing or not, and if you aren't performing, your customers will vote with their feet. The market decides whether you are worthy of bank funding, and if not, you will find yourself with 'more month than money'. The market also decides whether you are a good employer or not, and you'll find it extremely difficult to recruit the best talent if this goes against you.

## Other key differences

That's the biggest difference between employment and being your own boss, but it's the first of many.

### Finances

By being your own boss, you'll need to manage your financial situation, as there is no guaranteed pay cheque at the end of the month.

Instead, you will need to cater for seasonal fluctuations in your business, and the risk that you may lose some major customers overnight. You'll also need to cover your tax liabilities, as these won't be deducted from your pay cheque. This is often an eye-opener to most new business owners, who are used to living month to month on what their employer pays them.

## Customers

Next up, you will need to be responsible for finding and keeping customers. In an employed role, you will have support in this. Even if you are at the sharp edge of a sales team, you will still have a marketing team providing supporting material, and the business owner providing a vision and a strategy. In your own business, that's all down to you. As is keeping the admin side of things in order. And keeping the customers happy.

## Competition

You will also be more exposed to competition. In an employed role, you might find that you have competition for promotion with some of your colleagues. Depending on the type of business, you might find that this introduces office politics, or other detrimental behaviours. In business, the floor opens. Anyone providing the same service or product as you could theoretically be your competition. You will have people trying to be better than you, quicker than you and cheaper than you. And if they succeed, you feel it in your pocket straight away.

So there's the downsides! There are some benefits as well.

## Management

I'm sure some of you reading this have worked for *that* type of manager. You know the one that I mean. The jobsworth who obsesses over details for the sake of it. The micro-manager who might as well do the job themselves because they know best.

Or even worse, *the other* type of manager. The one who goes against the rule book, just to help themselves. Rather than praise in public and criticize in private, they just tread on whoever they need to, just to get their next promotion. Every good idea is their idea, and every problem is someone else's fault. Ownership of a task is a rarity; in fact, delegation – or abdication – is key to their success.

By being your own boss, you can choose which of these you want to be. Or of course, you can choose to do it properly.

## Strategy, control and choice

You'll also be able to control your own destiny. You will be in control of what you earn, the hours that you work, the type of work that you do, the type of business that you work in, the type of customer that you work for, and the way that you do what you do. You will be in control of your working environment, your schedule, and can even choose your preferred brand of coffee.

Taking these choices to another level, you will be in control of your company culture, your systems and processes, your management structure, the growth methodology, the number of employees you have, the equity funding that your corporation can raise, and your net worth at retirement.

Business ownership actually opens up a world of control, which can be quite daunting for those who are used to being managed and employed. With that comes a lot of responsibility, and the need for resilience and inner strength.

---

### A moment to reflect

Think about when you have been motivated at work. Was it down to a good manager who encouraged you? Was it down to positive feedback from a customer?

The reality of owning your own business is that motivation will have to come from you, and radiate from you to your team when you start employing people. Be honest with yourself: do you see the glass as half full or half empty? How will you drag yourself up when the pressure knocks you down? Do you have support outside of the business?

## *Motivation, validation and goal-setting*

If you've spent some time reflecting on the last action point, you will no doubt have considered how you are motivated. There's a general theme that people are motivated by the 'carrot' or the 'stick' – they either move towards the carrot, or away from the stick. If you've ever read a self-help or personal development book, you've undoubtedly come across that concept before. If you're anything like the audiences that I've spoken to across the world, you probably are already glossing over this paragraph, thinking that you are motivated by the carrot.

*Are you sure?*

### Carrot and stick

Take a step back for a moment, and think about how you're *really* motivated. Most people automatically say that they are motivated by the carrot, simply because that's what society expects of us. We see go-getters who appear to be focused on bigger and better cars, nicer watches and lofty financial goals. I would argue that in reality, most of us are actually motivated by the stick.

Don't believe me? Ask yourself these questions:

- At school/college, did you ever 'cram' at the last minute for an exam?
- Did you ever stay up late to finish a project?
- Have you ever put something off until next week/month/year?
- Have you ever had a health scare which has encouraged you to make changes in your life?
- Do you file your tax returns early?

You don't need me to tell you whether you should be answering yes or no to the above, or giving you some kind of score. Unless you have truly super-human motivation, it's likely that at least one of the above answers has demonstrated that *some* of your motivation comes from the stick, rather than the carrot. Every area in which we procrastinate would be easier in some way if we didn't – we would be more relaxed for our exams, be more prepared for our tax liabilities, or avoid the health scares completely. The reality is that we sometimes need a nudge to make things happen.

Stepping away from the binary view of carrot versus stick, we should also consider that we might approach different things in different ways. For example, we might proactively decide to do things that we enjoy, while putting off things that seem mundane. That's completely ordinary behaviour! But, when running a business, we need to acknowledge that there will be things that we have to do which we love doing, and things that need doing that we can't stand.

## Achievement goals and avoidance goals

Let's look at this from a practical perspective now. We've already seen that most people have a mix of motivations, and that predominantly, most people are at least partly motivated by the stick. What does that mean in reality for our businesses? Think about how most goals are set. Again, if you are like most people, a list of new year's resolutions might be:

- Lose 6 pounds of weight by March.
- Put aside 10 per cent of my income into a pension fund every month.
- Quit smoking immediately.
- Reduce alcohol consumption to weekends only.
- Learn a new language to a conversational level before our summer holiday.
- And so on...

These goals seem perfectly reasonable, right? We've all done it, haven't we? We set goals that seem to fit all of the usual criteria – they are specific, measurable, attainable, relevant and time-bound (SMART)... but when it comes to implementing them, there's one fundamental problem with goals that we have set in this way.

Goals like these are all based around the carrot. They are all focused on what we want to *achieve*, rather than what we want to *avoid*.

The problem with these goals is not the goals themselves. Of course, any goal that we set will be an 'achievement' goal. Very few of us would willingly aim towards something that isn't an achievement! The problem is the context that we put around them, and how we set out to achieve them. We look at implementing an achievement goal by taking a first step of achievement, and then another, and then another. Without consequence.

For those of us who are motivated by the stick, this method doesn't work.

---

### A moment to reflect

Think about how you are motivated. You might have instinctively answered 'carrot' before, but is that really right? And regardless of whether you are carrot or stick, do your goals support both methods of motivation and accountability? If you require a little stick to get things done, how can you introduce this into your planning and goal-setting?

---

## Internal and external validation

It's also worth considering the two different types of individual validation. Some of us are more externally motivated; that is, we tend to rely on feedback and being patted on the back when we do a good job. Others are more internally motivated. We tend not to need others to tell us that we are doing well, instead we know within ourselves that all is just fine. This will differ for all of us in certain environments, and indeed based on our own stress levels and mental health – but it is worth considering where you sit on this scale.

Again, this is a common area where people tend to misjudge themselves. At least, that is what I've seen from working with thousands of business owners and speaking to many more. Whenever I ask for a show of hands from an audience, just like with the carrot/stick question, I see everyone claiming that they are internally motivated. This is the case across the globe, and across various different types of audience. I have to smile, particularly if I see them sat there with overtly branded designer gear, or making a point of showing off their latest smartphone! It simply isn't true for everyone.

Just like the carrot/stick question, there is no right or wrong answer. The likelihood is that everyone will be motivated by some combination of carrot and stick, in different contexts; and that everyone will need some combination of internal and external validation in different contexts too. The key is that you answer it correctly *for yourself*, rather than how you believe that you need to be seen to answer. Once you know the real answer (not the one you 'ought' to give), you can then work out how best to frame your goals.

So, as a rather flippant example, I can confirm that for most things, I'm motivated by the stick, and am very externally motivated. Therefore, a *really* good way for me to achieve a goal – say, of 'losing 6 pounds by March' – is to post it on social media with some embarrassing pictures, with a statement that if I'm seen to eat any cake, my followers have permission to publicly shame me as it happens. This ticks the boxes of both external motivation and avoiding some introduced pain in one status update!

## A moment to reflect

Now you know how you are motivated, think about how you are validated. Do you need to make your intentions public? If you do, just a word of caution – make sure you balance commercial sensitivity with the need for external motivation. It's not always wise to shout before you start, particularly if you're sat on some trade secrets or non-compete agreements!

# What makes a successful business

Now that we've looked at what makes a successful business owner, we can look at what makes a successful business. If you ask any friends about what it is that makes a business successful, you'll hear a number of comments, both positive and negative, and considered from a variety of viewpoints:

*A new invention which everyone needs.*

*An inspirational entrepreneur at the top.*

*Owned by someone with a wealthy upbringing.*

*Being in the right place at the right time.*

*A product that I/my spouse like(s).*

*A business that balances profit and social responsibility.*

*A business that creates jobs.*

*etc...*

While these might all be valid for the person who makes the comment, they aren't the only ways to be successful. All of these things will help you in business, especially if your friend happens to also want your product that they/their spouse like! But businesses can prosper even without a new invention, without an inspirational entrepreneur, without family money, and so on. Sometimes, businesses are just an iteration or a slight improvement on what is being done already.

## *Dream, plan, do, review*

There are four steps that I would suggest make a business successful, which are all down to the business owner. These steps are shown in the following Figure:

DREAM    PLAN    DO    REVIEW

**Dream** – can you create a dream, and in turn a vision, which can stand up in a crowded marketplace and sustain the business through the short, medium and long term? Is the dream big enough and compelling enough to continually motivate the team, funders, customers, and you?

**Plan** – can you distil a dream into a structure, and create an actionable plan that can be implemented, together with the processes and systems to help the business succeed?

**Do** – can you actually take action? More importantly, *will* you take action?

**Review** – the final step of a cyclical process, revisiting the Dream, the Plan and the Do. Was the dream big enough? Was the plan actionable and correctly structured in accordance with the dream? Did you actually do what you planned to do?

It's really that simple! Every business failure that I've seen has come down to a failing in either the Dream, the Plan, the Do or the Review. These four steps quite clearly apply at the start of a business, but also apply at every stage of a business. I've found that business tends to be cyclical, and business owners need to revisit their dream, their plan, their actions and their accountability over and over again to ensure that they are still on track.

Something might jump out at you if you've been paying attention throughout the whole book. The analysis of Entrepreneur, Manager and Technician in *The E-Myth Revisited*, referred to in Chapter 1, fits in quite nicely here:

The Entrepreneur in us is responsible for the Dream.

The Manager in us is responsible for the Plan.

The Technician in us is responsible for the Do.

**And every bit of us is accountable during the Review.**

Unfortunately, there is no hiding from the fact that we need to step out of our comfort zones in business. While we might be most comfortable as a Technician, we need to adopt the roles of Entrepreneur and Manager as well. This requires both motivation and effort, to make sure that the business has the greatest chance of success.

> There's no point dreaming if you aren't going to plan and then do.
> A plan without a dream, or without action, is pointless.
> Action without structure or strategy is sometimes worse than inaction.
> And failing once is an error. Failing the same way twice is a mistake.

## Where it goes wrong

I'm going to spoil the surprise by telling you now about the area where most business owners fall down. Very simply, they don't get around to doing enough. They have a big idea – big enough to become a dream, and to motivate them to leave their job. They prepare business plans, set up 'funnels' and ad campaigns online, type out lots of financial projections and create CRM systems... but they don't actually pick up the phone and speak to potential customers. Usually the concepts are pretty good, the plans are optimistic but achievable, but the implementation is where it all falls down. They have instead indulged in 'creative avoidance' – doing anything but the important stuff.

---

### A moment to reflect

Think about how you are going to hold yourself accountable. You won't have a manager breathing down your neck, or a colleague waiting for you to finish your part of the process. How are you going to make sure that you do what you say you are going to do, and not succumb to doing something easier or more fun?

---

Provided you get the four steps correct, even the worst business model can limp along. You really don't need to reinvent the wheel to have a successful business. Google was just an improved version of Yahoo, Lycos and the numerous other search engines before it. It just did the job quicker, with a simplified interface. Apple, for all its innovation, rarely creates a new market. They just tend to do the proven stuff better than the early players, and market it to the masses.

## Innovation and unicorns

In fact, this brings us nicely on to innovation, and whether it is needed in your business. With the masses of innovation happening in the world right now, you'd be forgiven for thinking that businesses have to innovate to survive. That might be true to some extent, but certainly not at the expense of a stable business model. Businesses like Tesla might thrive on innovation, but the reality is that only a very small percentage of businesses would be able to do the same. The public perception, however, is that businesses need to innovate and create something new to survive. Why is this?

Very simply, it comes down to the 'unicorn' factor. For those that haven't heard this term used in a business context, a unicorn is a tech startup that reaches a $1 billion valuation, as measured by the valuation used for a fund raise. These businesses tend to be extremely innovative, and because of the combination of big numbers and new technology, also tend to garner a disproportionate level of press coverage. What we tend to forget when reading about these companies is that the vast majority of companies actually prop up the global economy without coming anywhere near the valuations or the innovations of these unicorns. We'll cover innovation in more detail within the next chapter, but please rest assured that your business can do just fine without the types of innovation that might immediately come to mind.

# Is success what it seems?

So far in this chapter, I've been referring to success in a very generic way, without attaching any connotations to the word 'success' apart from the survival of the business. A trap that I often see business owners fall into is the pursuit of what they superficially believe success to be, without consideration of what success really means to them.

In the next chapter, we'll cover business goal-setting in a lot more detail, and look in particular at why businesses tend not to hit their goals. Before even considering what your business goals should be, though, you should first step back and consider what success means to you.

Is success having a Lamborghini parked on the driveway? Is success summed up by a mansion overlooking the coast? Or, is success having a happy family? Being able to spend time with your friends or on the golf course? Reaching the age of 90 with plenty of fight left in you?

There are a number of ways of determining success, and often excelling in one area of your life comes at the detriment of others. It's always important to remember that there are no right or wrong answers, and you shouldn't do what you think society expects of you – only you can set your own ideas of success, based on what drives you forward and what you want to achieve.

A common tool used in life coaching circles is known as the Wheel of Life.[1] It summarizes several factors, including money, relationships, spirituality, health and so on. By doing this, individuals often notice that they haven't focused holistically on themselves. In fact, I tend to see areas that are maybe half the rating of others, meaning that there are imbalances between the various areas that contribute to a great life. If you get a chance, I strongly suggest that you take the opportunity to complete the Wheel of Life diagram for yourself to see how you score. Simply put, if you have big differences in your scores on the Wheel of Life, it's likely that you are in for a bumpy ride.

## A moment to reflect

What does success look like for you? Is it based on a financial target, a health target, a lifestyle target, or a relationship target? Or is it a combination of factors? Don't worry, there are no right or wrong answers – unless you're working towards someone else's success.

## Chapter 2 summary

In this chapter, we have looked at what it is that makes a business successful. It's a mixture of the resilience of the entrepreneur, the way that the entrepreneur motivates themselves, and the adherence to the simple steps which create and sustain businesses of all shapes and sizes.

Before proceeding to the next chapter, you should:

1 Think about all of the reflective questions within the chapter.

2 Download and review the Chapter 2 supplementary material from www.carlreader.com/bossit

3 Answer the following questions:

- How am I motivated?
  - *Carrot/Stick*

- How am I validated?
  - *Internal/External*

- How will I make my goals work for me?

  _____

  _____

  _____

  _____

## 03
# How to create a business idea

In this chapter you will:

- find out what makes a good idea;
- understand more about innovation and its place in business;
- learn why most business goals are destined for failure;
- find out how to tackle your limiting factors.

In the last chapter, we covered a fair bit of ground. We've looked at the motivations behind making the leap from a career into self-employment, and we've also looked at what makes a business work from a very high level. We'll be covering the various stages of the successful business cycle (Dream, Plan, Do and Review) in far more detail, but at this stage it is important just to understand the key principles and the fact that a business relies on all parts of this process being adhered to.

This chapter is really going to focus on the Dream part of the equation – and more specifically, looking at how to create a clear vision for a business rather than a disjointed jumble of ideas.

I'll start with the biggest killer at the Dream stage.

Very simply: entrepreneurs don't dream big enough.

# Dream big

So many business owners start with preconceived limitations. They don't believe that they will find enough customers. They think that their product can only be made in the way it's always been made. They think that their competitors today will be their competitors tomorrow. They think that other people have it easy.

This might seem surprising, particularly if you picture the stereotypical entrepreneur as a go-getting daydreamer. But it's true. This is exactly what so many business owners think, deep down. And these limitations permeate through their vision, their plans and their actions.

The end result of this is that business owners get trapped in a rat race of their own. Much like those in an employed career, they get out of bed having hit the snooze button several times, they drag themselves to the shower and then travel during rush hour to clock in at their workplace on time. The dream often seems like a distant past.

But the strange part of this whole story is that often, the entrepreneur has got pretty much what they wanted. The business is almost exactly how they envisioned it. They are working for the same kinds of customers that they dreamed of, just a few less. They are doing the same things that they thought they would be, just a bit less systemized and firefighting just a bit more. Everything is broadly the same, give or take a little.

The dream isn't in the past – it simply wasn't enough.

As humans, we all grow and develop. We might see the most dramatic physical and mental growth during our early years, and we might see some decline in certain areas at the end of our years. But as a rule, we tend to learn new things, have new experiences, and want to progress in areas that we are capable of progressing throughout our lives.

To keep ourselves growing as entrepreneurs, we need our businesses to grow at the same rate. What might seem daunting at the outset will soon seem like business as normal. What will appear to be big monthly numbers in the early days could soon become daily takings.

This idea links back quite nicely to the reasons why people start a business. Imagine this: you might feel trapped in your career. The glass ceiling is unfortunately only too common, particularly as businesses tend to operate in a pyramid structure. There are fewer places as you progress through an organization, and subconscious bias of all kinds can kick in. Even if you are fortunate enough to work for a truly equal opportunities employer, you'll still be up against your peers for progression. And your ultimate progression will be capped by the owner of the business, the board of directors, or the risk appetite of the shareholders – not to mention the difficulties in turning a huge corporate ship in a new direction.

So, in order for a dream to be good enough to build a business on, it needs to fit the following criteria:

- **big enough** to keep you motivated;
- **relevant** to both your definition of success and your personal values;
- **understandable** to team members, customers, suppliers and the wider world.

You'll see that there's no space for realism in the list above! Effective entrepreneurial dreaming focuses on the future, not the present. It's important to remove all preconceived limitations of technology, time and money. Instead, you need to think about what you would do if money was no object, and if you had the finest talent at your disposal. Entrepreneurial dreaming is about seeing what other people don't (or can't) see.

Your dream may be as simple as earning £50,000 rather than £30,000 in a similar career, while spending four days a week on a golf course. This dream is no less valid than – and could shatter as many limitations as – someone else's dream of running a multi-million-pound corporation based on systems, processes and new technology. Each example will require a new way of working, a new way of leveraging other people and a new way of systemizing what you do. Each will require an entrepreneurial way of thinking, dreaming and implementation. The only question left is how far you want to take the business to fit your own goals.

## A moment to reflect

What is it that holds you back in your dreaming? Do you worry about how you can afford to build the business? Do you just doubt yourself? Are you worried about how others will judge you and your dreams? Think about why you are holding yourself back, and consider whether there are other ways of approaching your dreams.

# Dream for yourself

Many, many business targets are doomed from the moment that they are set. It's not because the goals are too big – as we've seen, the bigger the better when it comes to dreaming – or because of any external limitations such as funding. Even if your dream *is* big enough, though, it's never going to work if goals for your business are not aligned with your personal goals.

Often, entrepreneurs believe that they have to think in a certain way. They think that they have to strive for a Ferrari, and that a high level of revenue is the single marker of their success. Logically, we might know that this is incorrect; however, so often we still set targets based on what we think should be expected of us.

This is completely understandable. Our society has a tendency to condition us in a certain way, which is often a great thing. Norms and expectations, and a certain level of conformity, are necessary for a functional society! What's interesting, though, is that those who *do* branch out from societal norms still tend to follow the norms expected for their own path. There are many examples of this: people who decide to go travelling generally tend to visit the same regions as each other; people living a life of crime tend to follow similar paths. And entrepreneurs, who also branch out from societal norms, tend to follow the path that they believe other entrepreneurs follow. The dreams that they set aren't their dreams.

> ## A moment to reflect
>
> What do you *really* want? We focused on the definitions of success in the last chapter; now think about whether the definitions that you've set for yourself are truly owned by you. What are your personal values? What do you stand for in life? What is the most important thing in your life? Does the 'success' that you considered before sit alongside your values and paradigms?

## *Conflicting goals*

When you have two compelling goals that are headed in different directions, there is only one end result that can come from it. You will either fail at one of them, or (more likely) fail at both of them. Whatever the particulars, the end result is failure.

That might seem very dramatic, but it does need to be said. An admittedly extreme example of what I'm talking about might be someone who wants to retire to a sunny resort within a year, while also building a multi-million-pound empire and increasing their personal net worth by several zeroes. Neither goal is unrealistic in its own right, but when combined, the incompatibility of the two targets will only lead to disappointment and – ultimately – failure. In order for our imaginary entrepreneur to have any chance of success, the reality is that one of these goals will have to shift.

You shouldn't use this as a reason not to think big, though. It is possible to build a big business – thousands and thousands have done it before. It is also possible to build a lifestyle business, and fund your dream life in that sunny destination. You just need to work out what it is that you really want, and drill into both your personal and business goals to make sure that they are aligned. It's all about the relevance of your business goals to your personal values and desires.

# Dream clearly

For those of you who paid attention earlier in this chapter, you'll remember that there is a third element to a strong entrepreneurial dream: the ability to communicate it easily, so that people such as customers, investors and potential staff can understand it.

I can't count the number of times I've been left confused by a business idea; it has either been too complicated, too clouded by detail, or just way over my head from a technical complexity and jargon perspective. Of course, while I personally might not be someone that you need to persuade, you will have staff, customers, suppliers, funders and a wider world that you *will* need to buy into your vision. Make sure that you can sum your business up simply and succinctly, so that you can engage anyone and everyone into what it is that you see.

## Examples of great dreams

Here are a couple of case studies of larger corporate businesses and their stated visions. Even though your business might play on a much smaller scale than these enterprises, we can learn from the simplicity of their approach, and the sheer refusal to accept any societal norms.

**CASE STUDY**   Tesla

*Tesla's mission is to accelerate the world's transition to sustainable energy.[1]*

For me, this statement sums up exactly what Tesla are trying to achieve. It is certainly not limited in any way, shape, or form: we can see how this vision plays out in their business by what they've done with their development of vehicles, and the later projects that Elon Musk has embarked on (such as Solar Roof and Gigafactory). In terms of congruity with the founder's values, it is clearly in alignment with what Musk is trying to achieve, given his drive to move the world away from fossil fuels. Finally, it has been communicated in a way that an eight-year-old can understand.

## CASE STUDY   Canva

*Empowering everyone to create beautiful designs without friction.[2]*

Canva started from an e-book creation tool,[3] but before long Melanie Perkins realized the product that her team had on their hands. Back in 2007, anyone looking to design something on their computer was stuck between the simple and the complicated! The choice available was pretty much a two-horse race between the Adobe suite of professional grade products and Microsoft Paint. Anyone looking to use a product that could create professional graphics had a steep learning curve, and a significant investment in high-level software. Perkins experienced this first hand, while she was studying at the University of Western Australia, teaching students how to use Adobe products.[4] This vision, while ambitious, shaped the direction of Canva as a freemium online design tool that is simple to use yet highly effective.

## CASE STUDY   Nike

*Bring inspiration and innovation to every athlete\* in the world. (\*If you have a body, you are an athlete.)[5]*

I'm sure it's hard for many of us to remember a time before Nike. What is now a clear market leader in sports apparel was once a young upstart, competing with the likes of Adidas. (Interesting side note – back in the 1960s, their vision was simply 'Crush Adidas'.)[6] Nike had a clear aim of empowering everybody to become an athlete in their own way, and supported this through their advertising campaigns, which demonstrated that every piece of tarmac could be a running track, and their sponsorship of athletes. Notably, they sponsored athletes that were relatable to the general public, and now they are one of the first ports of call for budding athletes everywhere.

**CASE STUDY**   Amazon

*To be Earth's most customer-centric company, where customers can find and discover anything they might want to buy online, ... [at] the lowest possible prices.*[7]

Finally, we can look at Amazon's dream, stated back in 1995. Bear in mind that this was set when the internet was in its infancy, and the possibility of global e-commerce wasn't even in the minds of most of the world. The world's first secure online retail transaction had taken place less than 12 months previously, and the internet had just seen its first ever banner advert. Not to mention the fact that at this point, you'd have struggled to find much more than a relatively small selection of books on Amazon's website at this time. Again, from Jeff Bezos we have global ambitions, without limits. His dream was crystal clear, and is just as relevant today as it was back then.

While we said that your business might be on a smaller scale than these examples, I'd be pretty sure that the description of your dream is a little longer! Think about how these entrepreneurs have managed to capture their global transformational dreams in a single sentence or two.

## A moment to reflect

Take a moment to think about your business. Your dreams are probably a lot fuzzier than the snappy one-liners described above. Where is your future market (regional, national, international)? Who is your customer? What are you offering them? How do you impact their lives? What fundamental change will you deliver that no one else will? These questions can help form the basis of your dream.

# Innovation

But, don't I have to innovate…? To a point, yes. All businesses need to innovate to survive. But the innovation that you think that you need isn't necessarily the innovation that you *actually* need.

The word 'innovation' captures a wide range of activities. It encompasses everything from research through to breakthroughs. An iterative upgrade to an iPhone could be deemed an innovation, just as a new invention of a method of instant travel across the world would be. A discovery of a cure for cancer is innovation, just in the way that a discovery of a new road to be drawn onto a map could be an innovation in the cartographic world. The difference between these innovations comes down to the impact level of the innovations, and the way in which they are uncovered (accidentally versus deliberate).

## *The different types of innovation*

A great way of thinking about innovation is to consider it in the context of the four types of innovation, as categorized by Greg Satell in his book *Mapping Innovation: A playbook for navigating a disruptive age.*[8]

### Research

At its simplest, innovation is research, as performed in universities across the world. There is little focus to the problem that is trying to be solved, and the domain in which the problem lies. This kind of innovation isn't particularly targeted, but some great things can come out of research.

Some examples of products that this kind of innovation might lead to:

- university research;
- IBM/research labs.

## Breakthrough innovation

Moving on, there is breakthrough innovation, where there is a strong definition of the problem being solved. It could be the combination of three devices into one, like the iPhone, or perhaps the elimination of fossil fuels.

Some examples of products that this kind of innovation might lead to:

- Tesla cars;
- Apple iPhone.

## Disruptive innovation

Then we have disruptive innovation, where a user base is fairly well defined, but the problem isn't. This could be the iPod Shuffle. It's a perfect idea in principle – it was cheaper than an iPod, smaller than an iPod and perfect for the gym. Great concept, but not a great long-term seller. Whenever I speak about innovation, everyone remembers it, but no one remembers where they left it. The problem that it solved wasn't painful enough and big enough for the innovation to stick.

Some examples of products that this kind of innovation might lead to:

- Amstrad eMailer;
- Apple iPod Shuffle.

## Sustaining innovation

The majority of business innovation is in fact sustaining innovation, where the problem to be solved is very well defined, and the domain in which you're working is also really well defined.

Some examples of products that this kind of innovation might lead to:

- upgrades to the Apple iPhone;
- new models of PlayStation and Xbox.

## *Innovate to your strengths*

Tim Kastelle,[9] a leading author and commentator on innovation, contends that 70 per cent of a business's innovation should focus on its existing markets and existing technology (effectively, it's existing business), 20 per cent should focus on existing business that is being served by a competitor or by other technology, and only 10 per cent on opening new markets and developing new technology – based on the three horizons model from *The Alchemy of Growth*.[10]

The point is this: innovation doesn't need to be groundbreaking to be successful. When we look at technology such as televisions and other domestic appliances, for example, what was once a product cycle counted in years may well now be counted in months, and we are increasingly living in a world that changes quickly. Each new iteration is an opportunity for small, impactful innovations.

It also isn't all about products, despite these being the first thing that comes to mind when we think about innovation. Service and delivery can also be subject to innovation. Businesses need to innovate to stay fresh, but they don't need to break new barriers every five minutes – instead, sustaining innovation can keep them relevant and 'in the game'.

So what does this mean for a new business? Simply, you just need to innovate in some way, shape, or form – but not necessarily how you perceive that other businesses innovate. You need to provide an iterative improvement, either internally (within the operations of your business) or externally (how your customers perceive your business). This will be your differentiator, and might indeed become your unique selling proposition (USP). Just as Google became the fastest search engine, or Amazon became the 'everything store', you should look at how you can start and rapidly improve your business. This falls firmly within sustaining innovation, and it's important that sustaining innovation forms part of your day-to-day business procedures. The rest is nice to have, but not always the most important thing to be focusing on in the early days.

**A moment to reflect**

Think about how you are going to innovate. Is your new business based on some new technology that is yet to be built, or a simple improvement on an existing business model? How will you ensure that you continue to be on top of your game? What kind of innovation is needed to fulfil your ultimate dream? This will form part of your planning, which we will cover in later chapters.

# Creating your unique selling proposition (USP)

A USP is what sets a business apart from its competitors. If you cannot describe your USP, you will find it difficult to attract customers, staff and funders. Even if you are a sole proprietor, you need to work out what it is that you do differently, and how to promote it to the outside world.

Let's take an example. Imagine you're a decorator. You're currently employed, and are frustrated with the way that your company does business. You hate leaving customers with what you feel is a sloppy job, and a bill that is much higher than expected. What's more, you don't see any of that high fee because you are paid an hourly rate. Enough is enough! You decide to set up on your own. You make a commitment to only charge on a fixed-fee basis, rather than by the hour. Once you've quoted an amount, you commit to it. You'll use the highest levels of protection on the floors and offer a 'no spill guarantee'. Those two service differentiators will lead towards your USP and should set you apart from other decorating companies.

You've also thought about the future of decorating as an industry, and decided that you need to keep on top of what's happening in the wider world. You know that DIY stores are offering 'mess free' painting products, and customers might feel that they can do what you're offering by themselves, and you've also got your guarantee to live up to – so, it might be that you decide to attend trade shows and use the latest tools and methods to help you live up to your standards, and offer a better option than DIY. You might also decide to buy a route mapping service, so that your customers can find out exactly when you will be arriving, by text message. Not only will these things continue to add to your USP, but will also be an investment in 'sustaining innovation'. You aren't reinventing the wheel, but you are keeping on top of changes and trends.

For most businesses, their USP lies in how they do it – the 'internal' operations that set them apart from other companies – or in what they do for their customers – the 'external' selling proposition. I've listed a few ideas in Table 3.1 to help you to start thinking about where your USP could lie in comparison with other businesses.

You'll see in the examples in Table 3.1 that some internal factors of your USP naturally lead to external factors; and some desired external factors may prompt you to work on internal matters to be able to achieve them. One thing that is important to remember is the U in USP – Unique. If your USP is something that is considered to be industry standard, it's not a USP worth shouting about. There's only one way to find out if your offering is truly unique, and that's research! We cover research in a little more depth when we talk about your business plan, but in the meantime a quick search online will give you some clues about what your competitors are doing. Usually, if a business has a genuine USP, they shout from the rooftops about it!

## A moment to reflect

Not all USPs are truly appreciated by the business owner. A great example of this is in the film *The Founder*, which shows a dramatized version of the McDonald's story. The original founders of the business were so busy making their burgers quickly and consistently, when compared with a traditional diner, that they didn't realize what an asset they were sat on. While I'm sure the film was exaggerated for cinematic impact, we probably all know local businesses who are doing amazing things or offering a great service, but they simply don't shout about it.

**Table 3.1** Internal and external USPs

| | |
|---|---|
| **Examples of internal USPs** | *Technological advancements* – you may have market-leading technology, either self-built or purchased.<br><br>*Robust processes and procedures* – you may have invested time in ensuring that your processes are as efficient as possible.<br><br>*Buying power/economies of scale* – you may be able to buy your stock cheaper than others.<br><br>*Contacts* – you might simply have a better 'black book' than your competitors.<br><br>*Exclusive distributorships* – you may be the only one able to buy your stock in a region. |
| **Examples of external USPs** | *Sales channels* – you may have the opportunity to sell your product in supermarkets, or fit the right criteria to sell your services into certain corporates or the public sector.<br><br>*Speed* – you may be able to turn around your service more quickly than other businesses.<br><br>*End price* – you may be able to produce your goods or price your services cheaper than your competitors.<br><br>*Convenience* – you might be able to offer your customers more convenience, perhaps by visiting their homes in an unserved region, or through online offerings.<br><br>*Service* – you may offer a personal service that bigger businesses just can't. |

Your USP also then allows you to think about your 'elevator pitch'. This isn't an excuse to create a sales pitch, but instead is an opportunity to summarize your business in a compelling fashion, in just a couple of sentences. A perfect way of creating an elevator pitch is to focus on your customer-facing USP, and the benefits that your customers receive. So, rather than describing yourself as 'a decorator with 15 years' experience who prides themselves on their work' (you-focused), you can be 'a decorator who transforms rooms, at a fixed price with a no-quibble money-back guarantee' (customer-focused). Who would you rather do business with?

---

### A moment to reflect

How is your customer going to benefit from your business? How are you different? What is your dream? What is your USP? And how will you communicate that in an elevator pitch?

---

# Limiting factors

All of this talk about big dreams, goals and innovations is great, but the reality is that you will have some limitations to your business. It could be a lack of staff, a lack of money, or indeed the fear of the unknown: every business has limiting factors, and the sign of a strong entrepreneur is the ability to identify these issues and work out a way to overcome them.

Limiting factors broadly fall into two camps: internal limiting factors and external limiting factors. External limiting factors are the ones that are out of your control, such as market size, technological capacities, or customer demand. The only way that you can overcome these is by growing your dream or changing the way that you do things.

## Internal limiting factors

The factors that you can have far more control over are the internal factors, which are matters that lie either within the business, or in the mind of the entrepreneur.

The sub-division between the internal limiting factors is important as we need to approach them in a different way. We also need to be conscious of when a psychological limiting factor is appearing to create a business limiting factor. A great example of this, which I see time and time again, is the fear of taking on external funding.

We'll go into far more detail about funding in a later chapter, but for now: let's imagine a company that needs to take on some debt to fund its working capital. The numbers stack up, the business is going well despite some cash flow issues, and the bank would probably be prepared to lend the money. On paper, there are no issues here whatsoever, and the working capital gap can be easily plugged.

If only!

Let's take a deeper look into the mindset of the entrepreneur. Let's just imagine that this entrepreneur had grown up in a household where debt was frowned upon. They were warned against borrowing money from friends to buy the latest toy, with sayings such as 'neither a borrower nor a lender be'. Their parents regaled tales of friends and associates who had run up debts through gambling and reckless spending. They received some offers of credit cards as soon as they turned 18, but were just as quickly reminded of the downward spiral that some people take when tempted by the plastic.

Do you think this entrepreneur would be keen to take on debt in their business, despite it being a logical solution to their predicament?

This is just one example of the many ways that entrepreneurs can be limited by what they have heard or learned while growing up. Have you heard of any of the following phrases?

- 'Money can't buy you happiness.'
- 'Stocks and shares aren't for people like us.'
- 'You want to get a nice, secure 9–5 job.'
- 'He's just a typical salesman.'
- 'Rich people are greedy/selfish/crooks.'
- 'If you study hard and get good grades, you could work for a really good company.'

Every one of these phrases, and many, many more, could well be sat in the recesses of your mind, holding you back.

---

## A moment to reflect

Think about all the phrases, comments and experiences that you might have heard about money and business in your formative years – regardless of whether they were well intended. List them out and think logically about whether they are really something that you should hold with any level of regard. If you find any that you need to weed out, this is something that you can only do with conscious effort. Find any and every example where you can disprove your belief.

---

It's vital that you take some time reflecting on what could be holding you back. We can usually work around external limiting factors, as every other business has the same playing field as us to work within. We can overcome internal limiting factors if our head is in the right place, as we can make a plan to create the best outcome. But if our thinking isn't conducive to creating the plan, we'll never overcome the issues.

## Chapter 3 summary

In this chapter we have looked at how important it is to define your own business dream, rather than someone else's. We then looked at innovation, the role that this plays in most businesses, and took this one step further to look at how it can form part of your unique selling proposition. Finally, we looked at limiting factors, both real and perceived.

Before proceeding to the next chapter, you should:

1   Think about all of the reflective questions within the chapter.

2   Download and review the Chapter 3 supplementary material from www.carlreader.com/bossit

3   Answer these questions:

   o   What type of innovation will you focus on? (choose one)

      – *Research/Disruptive/Sustaining/Breakthrough*

   o   What is your unique selling proposition?

      _____

      _____

      _____

      _____

   o   What limiting factors do you have?

      _____

      _____

      _____

      _____

# Part Two
# Plan it

# 04
# From dreaming to planning

In this chapter you will:

- learn how to take your idea and distil it into a plan
- understand more about effective planning and target-setting
- learn how to create a business roadmap
- find out some basic project management ideas.

We've now completed Part One of this book, which is also part one of my model for building any business – you should be comfortable with your business dream and what you are trying to achieve. While it is important to continually revisit and improve your dream, there is also a point at which you have to take your dream and move it into something more concrete – the plan.

Planning is often the area where I see business owners let themselves down. Sometimes they use planning as a useful way of avoiding real work, and continually update their goal lists and business plans without taking action. Otherwise, they neglect the planning stage and dive straight into action, with no structure or logic behind their actions and activities. It's important to try to find a halfway house between these two approaches to give your business the best chance of success.

# What makes a strong plan?

When you think of a business plan, you probably think of a weighty document, perhaps with a glossy cover, or presented on PowerPoint slides by some high-flying executives. Well, it's true that the document you're thinking of is referred to as a 'business plan', but in this chapter we are actually looking at the whole planning process. Often the business plan is confused with a 'pitch deck', which is a business plan produced for investors or funders – essentially, a pitch deck, or a glossy-covered business plan report, is only one small use of a true business plan. A pitch deck might contain similar headings to a full business plan, but it is often used solely to get cash in the bank, rather than to set out the steps and targets for the business.

So, with that clear, let's focus on the whole process of planning. It's important to bear in mind that we all have our own approach to planning and structure. Personally, I tend to plan a little less formally than most, and I find that I tend to work better with a very broad big-picture plan, combined with very short-term detailed actions in alignment to the plan. Others prefer to work on a much more structured basis, perhaps tying daily actions into weekly targets, and in turn into monthly and quarterly goals.

## A moment to reflect

How do you tend to approach planning in your daily life? Do you have daily to-do lists, shopping lists and meal plans? Or do you have a more haphazard approach? Do you find that you enjoy working within a structured plan, or do you prefer to break the plan and see what works?

There is no one approach that works. What I'll describe here is what I see as best practice, but one thing more important than a plan is a plan that is actually used! If you feel that this approach to planning is too light-touch or overkill, then feel free to adapt the process to fit the way that you work. Perhaps the biggest problem with traditional business plans (or funding decks, as referred to above) is that they often end up gathering dust in a drawer somewhere, with no actionable steps, accountability, or proactive review and amendment. An effective plan for your business isn't constrained to a few PowerPoint slides; it should be a living document that grows with the business.

Presuming that a plan is actually used, there is another weakness that is rooted in the thinking of entrepreneurs and funders, and that is a disconnect between the dream and the results. Many people get excited by the dreams that are put forward in plans and focus their due diligence on the validation of the concept, reviews of the marketplace, and kicking the tyres of things like competitor analysis. The finance people will also have a keen eye on the numbers, making sure that revenue growth is both attractive and achievable, and trying to sense-check whether the entrepreneur has truly thought through the operating margins, overheads and the impacts on cash flow. This typical approach misses perhaps the most important part, which is how the results will be achieved.

Instead of focusing on just the 'why' and the 'what', we need to make sure that we cover the 'how' – how do we go from A to B, the practical steps that need to be taken, and some of the contingency plans that should be in place? In short, we need to plan our *actions*, not our *results*.

## Sensitivity analysis: having a backup plan

We'll cover the typical business plan/pitch deck structure in the next chapter, and that's where you'll find details of how to perform competitor analysis, and the types of numbers that funders look for. Here, we'll focus on the bigger picture – and one of those things is an understanding of what is and isn't within your control as an entrepreneur.

I mentioned before that plans tend to focus on the output of the business – who the business serves, the customer benefit and ultimately the return for the business owner and any shareholders. It's really important that this stuff is nailed down, but it is only part of the jigsaw. The performance of the business will be dependent both on the actions that are taken and the external matters that are outside of your control as a business owner.

Some of these are obvious and are covered by a typical 'PEST' (political, economic, societal and technological) review that would usually be included within a formal business plan. Things like political uncertainty, shifts in consumer behaviour, and technological developments can be predicted to an extent, and should be borne in mind when running the business. While these are all largely out of your control as a business owner, we often neglect to consider the risks closer to home. From a more hands-on perspective, we should also be thinking about the practical risks to the business of ill health, unexpected competition and things simply not going to plan. We'll touch on this more later in the chapter.

---

### Tip
What's plan B?

My recommendation for all planning processes is to think of plans B, C and D. While it might be Instagram-friendly to see motivational quotes with phrases such as 'No Plan B', the reality is that you owe it to yourself, your family and any future employees, customers, suppliers and funders to have a rounded plan of attack that covers different eventualities.

The formal phrase for having a range of backup plans is a 'sensitivity analysis'. In practice, this often looks like a broad adjustment to the financial forecasts of the business – for example, to see what would happen if revenues are 20 per cent lower than expected, or profit margins are 3 per cent lower. While adapting the results helps to sense-check the financial stability of the business, they don't actually help address the change in course required at an early point to limit the damage to the numbers.

Instead, I'd like you to bear the following in mind when creating your action plans:

**What if?** How do I keep my medium- to long-term targets flexible, in order to take advantage of new opportunities or threats? What is the process for this?

**Adaptation** How do I flex my short-term actions to take into account changes to the market, or simply learning new ways to do things? How will I review the changes to ensure that they tie back to my medium- to long-term targets?

**Protection** How do I protect the business from the unexpected, and mitigate any damage? Do I need to take preventative steps, find ways to structure the business so that I'm not the only source of income, or invest in insurance?

Another factor that the traditional sensitivity analysis doesn't really cover is the impact of timing. In my experience, tech businesses are particularly guilty of not hitting development milestones or revenue targets. It's all well and good having a beautiful set of projections that pass muster even with a large percentage tweak, but the reality is that the hidden killer in these sorts of businesses is the timeline.

When producing your plans, you need to think about the timeliness of your actions, and the impact of actions not being completed by a certain point. Can your business sustain itself if your website is one, three or six months late? What if employing your first member of staff takes longer to recruit than expected? Mapping out the impact of these potential delays can help you be prepared for the very worst case scenarios, and also help you understand the importance of certain actions compared with others.

# How do I begin the process of planning?

Traditional business plans are normally structured as words first, numbers second – and I'd strongly suggest that you take that approach as well. One of the temptations when preparing a business plan is to produce a 'spreadsheet millionaire' story. It might sound strange, but it's a trap I've seen so many business owners fall into! They want to justify why they are making this crazy step to their spouse, partner, neighbour, or anyone else who has heard the big picture dream. They use the numbers as a way of logically justifying their business; however, at this stage, if the written steps haven't been performed, the numbers are still just part of the emotional dream.

---

**Important!**

The business plan itself isn't the end goal here. Most of the planning benefit comes from going through the processes required to prepare the plan. The business plan itself helps you raise funds, and keeps you accountable down the line.

---

# Suggested structure of a business plan

When producing a formal business plan, you'd expect to include the following sections.

## The 'easy' bit

These sections of the business plan are reasonably self-explanatory, and if your dream is clear enough, you should have no difficulty in talking about what you are planning to do – this should just be a process of distilling your thoughts into words.

## Executive summary

Normally, this is a one-pager that explains the business concept and how much money is needed, in the hope that the bank manager would be tempted to turn to page 2. But as we know, we aren't just doing this to get some money from the bank! I'm still a big fan of producing this summary, though. It helps you ensure that your message, and the reason why your business will be a success, can be condensed into an easily digestible format. This will help you in your sales, your marketing, your recruitment… in fact, at any point that you need to talk about your business.

## Background of the business owner

Again, this is sometimes something that is squeezed in for the sake of it. Don't skip the work on this part, though; there's real value in taking the time to reflect on your own background. During this planning stage, focus on reviewing your weaknesses, rather than attempting to impress the bank manager with your direct industry experience. Have you had experience of sales, marketing, finance, administration, product creation, etc? Are you able to produce legal agreements, design your logo, code your website and manage your social media? The likelihood is that there will be some gaps in your experience – and also some unexpected wins (such as the amount of time that you've spent on Instagram…!). These gaps should form part of your action plan, where you will set tasks to either undergo some training or to recruit help from an employee or a consultant.

## Background of the team (if relevant)

If you are starting the business with more than one person, you should make sure that you also provide details of who they are and what they are bringing to the table. Perhaps you have a business partner, or a first employee already chosen. You might even want to include industry advisers and mentors in this section, as it will help you to understand what everyone is bringing to the table.

## Detailed description of the business

Now you can go wild! The kind of things I would expect to see in this section include: what you do, why you do it, how you do it and who you do it for. If you are running a technology business, you might want to think about going into some detail about the tech behind the scenes. Likewise, if you are producing products, this would be the ideal time to talk about any prototypes that you've had produced, your supply chain and any customer conversations that you've had so far. In an ideal world, you should get this section critically appraised by someone experienced in the business world. You want someone who is able to fulfil the hypothetical roles of bank manager, investor, customer, supplier and potential purchaser of the business. They will help you identify your blind spots – and once they're identified, you'll be able to decide whether the gaps can be filled simply by a clearer explanation in your plan, or whether you need to find a more substantial solution. Remember, this is the planning stage – don't be surprised if things come up that mean you need to go back to the drawing board or otherwise radically rethink your idea.

## *The slightly harder bit*

Now there are some further sections which require a lot more thought and research. Let's look at how to go about these in a bit more detail:

### Market research

This is where you 'kick the tyres' of your business idea – so to speak – and make sure that there are actually customers who are ready and willing to buy your product or service. This is vital: in my experience, a common and significant challenge faced by many new businesses is a misalignment between *what the business offers* and *what the market wants*.

It is possible to perform market research from the luxury of your living room, doing research via Google on your mobile phone.

And there's nothing wrong with this – it's a great place to start! I would, however, urge you to go into quite a bit more detail with your research than just that. There are two types of research – quantitative (based on facts and figures) and qualitative (based on feelings and emotions) – and a comprehensive market research approach should focus on both. Some methods of market research that I would look to employ for a new business might include:

- focus groups with potential customers;
- focus groups with other suppliers in the industry;
- counting footfall outside a retail location;
- observing typical customer spend trends in similar businesses;
- speaking to trade associations about your proposed business and the industry;
- participation in online communities where your potential customers are.

It might feel like overkill, but it's not simply enough to love your product or service. Instead, you need to love your target customer, and also try to get into their mindset as much as possible. By being able to empathize with their behaviours and actions, and the way in which they make purchasing decisions, you will be able to see clearly whether there is a product/market fit in your new venture.

## Competitor analysis

Much as you need to check that there is a market for your new business, you also need to have a real grasp on your competitors. In discussions with new business owners, I often find that they tend to have a rather dim view of their competitors. For example, a restaurant might look down on the quality of hamburgers served by McDonald's, without considering the business systems which allow them to do what they do with such consistency and at a global scale, or the wider market's desires.

This actually brings me to a related point which we need to always keep at the back of our minds. In Chapter 2, we talked about the 'technician' side to our personalities. The passion for what we do, and how we do it, is often one of the drivers that leads us towards starting our own business – but it can also be a limiting factor in the way that we view our own businesses, and our competitors. By dismissing some factors that might seem contrary to how we'd like our service or product to be delivered, we might very well miss the magic that makes those businesses special.

So, with a set of unbiased eyes, we need to look at who our competitors are, and how they are doing. This research can start with simple desk and observation research – walk down your local high street to find similar businesses, search online and ask friends. You will soon have a list of businesses that operate in a similar field to you. If you are looking at starting a tech startup, you may need to look on crowdfunding sites to see if there are any similar concepts; whereas if you are looking at restaurants, your competition may be a lot more visible and easy to find.

## Tip
Know your competition

Your competition may not look like you expect; don't limit your analysis to somebody doing exactly the same thing as you are planning to do. Take a moment to imagine that you are looking to set up a Vietnamese restaurant. Your competition isn't just other Vietnamese restaurants in your local area; it is actually *any other business* that competes for that section of consumer spend – so it is likely that you would include other cuisines, and potentially other activities, within your competitor analysis: fast food places; French or Italian or Mexican restaurants; even grocery delivery services which might cause people to stay in and cook instead of going out to eat.

Once you have an idea of who your competitors are, it's time to do some research on them! Much of the research will follow a similar pattern to the kind of research that you did for your market research – you can ask questions of focus groups, watch footfall in their stores, and understand the general feeling and sentiment around the business. I would, however, advise that you also consider more quantitative data, including publicly filed financial statements, independent review sites, and any other data that you can find. All of this will help you to understand how they are performing, and will either validate your own plans, or give you information to rethink.

## SWOT analysis

The final area of your plan that we will explore here is your SWOT analysis, which can be produced once you have performed your market research and competitor analysis.

The SWOT analysis is a commonly used model for analysing where a business is at any one point in time, and is simply a breakdown of the *Strengths*, *Weaknesses*, *Opportunities* and *Threats* facing a business. Let's break it down a little further:

Within your control –

- **Strengths:** these are the things that you excel at, and differentiate you in the market.
- **Weaknesses:** there are areas that you could improve on to benefit your offering.

Outside your control –

- **Opportunities:** these are the areas that you can benefit from in the future.
- **Threats:** these are external factors that might impact your business.

If you've been paying attention throughout the whole chapter, you'll have noticed that the external factors outside your own control (opportunities and threats) were referred to earlier, and the PEST model (political, economical, societal and technological) was suggested as a way of breaking them down and identifying them.

The production of a SWOT analysis is the first step towards using it for effective planning; simply going through the process of using the model is a hugely valuable exercise, providing you with lots of information and getting you used to the most effective ways of thinking about your business. However, doing a SWOT analysis and then just leaving it is obviously not using this tool to the best effect! I would recommend that you *know what you plan to do* with the results from the SWOT analysis. When used well, this should help you identify what you need to do to make your business a success. As a broad rule of thumb, you should look to:

- Play to your **strengths.**
- Patch up your **weaknesses.**
- Take advantage of your **opportunities.**
- Be mindful of, but not consumed by, your **threats.**

This is a tool that can be used for any business, and you might even find that you want to use this model on your key competitors, as part of your competitor analysis.

## PEST(LE) analysis

We've touched on the PEST analysis a couple of times in this chapter as it forms part of the SWOT analysis. I find that this is a very useful way of identifying the external factors (opportunities and threats) as it helps provoke thinking in different areas.

I've used PEST so far in this chapter; however, some prefer to break it down further into PESTLE – political, economical, societal, technological, legal and environmental. Whichever version you use is your own choice, provided that you remember to include legal and environmental factors within the PEST categories should you prefer to go down that route.

Some examples of the areas you may wish to think about in each section of this analysis are listed in Table 4.1 (those marked with * indicate items that may be explored further should you use the full PESTLE model).

**Table 4.1** PESTLE analysis

| Political | The stability of government and ability to make decisions<br>The direction of government and political opinion<br>Global trade and international agreements<br>Upcoming legislation (*)<br>Upcoming taxation policy (*) |
|---|---|
| **Economical** | Current economic conditions<br>Employment rates<br>Inflation rates<br>Consumer confidence<br>Upcoming taxation policy (*) |
| **Societal** | Lifestyle trends<br>Income distribution<br>Demographic influences and shifts<br>Media opinion and direction<br>Consumer attitudes and opinions (*) |
| **Technological** | Technological innovations<br>Technological awareness<br>Technology adoption and usage rates<br>User attitudes and opinions<br>Fiscal policy and taxation reliefs (*) |
| **Legal** | Employment legislation<br>Competition legislation<br>Consumer protection legislation<br>Intellectual property legislation<br>Taxation policy |
| **Environmental** | Environmental policies<br>Climate change<br>Reporting requirements<br>Weather and temperature changes<br>Corporate and social responsibility expectations |

As you can see, using this model helps you to expand your thinking around external factors – ensuring that your SWOT analysis is well thought through.

**Important!**

You can probably tell by now that there is a common theme in your business plan – research, research and more research is the key to success! You should be spending far more time than you might expect looking into your business, the industry that it will be in, and the environment that you'll be trading in. Asking the right questions now could well save you a lot of time and money down the line.

# What to do next with your business plan

So you have all these words typed up… now what? Once you have prepared these sections of the formal business plan, you can focus on producing the 'roadmap' for your business. More formally, we'd call this a project plan, setting out the key milestones together with a list of actions and accountabilities beneath.

I would imagine that from the business plan preparation, you have been left with at least a few actions that need to be undertaken. (If you haven't, you're either mind-blowingly overprepared and prescient, or you've not done as thorough a job as you need to!) These actions might be solved by some simple desk research using Google; however, it is likely that you may need to go a bit deeper in certain areas – perhaps you might need to find some expert advisers for some areas of your business, or produce a more rounded proposition so that the obvious questions that others may have are answered immediately.

Your roadmap should encompass everything that you need to do to take your business from where you are today to the fulfilment of your end goals. However, it is worth remembering that the roadmap will start as a detailed to-do list, and end as a very broad plan – the actions you note down will become less detailed the further into the future they are. This is completely natural, and is the reason why any business planning process needs to be continually revisited and refreshed. In fact, this is one of the main reasons that the Dream – Plan – Do – Review cycle ends with Review.

No two roadmaps will be the same, but broadly you should be covering the following areas:

- activities to be undertaken before fundraising;
- activities to be undertaken after fundraising;
- startup activities;
- activities to recruit first team member;
- scaling activities.

You might also find that your timeline differs – for example, you might not need to raise external funds to start the business, or you might need team members before you can open your doors to the public. The important thing here is to think about the broad stages, before you start planning the individual activities, so that you understand which activities depend on others to be completed. This planning process will help you avoid being overwhelmed, as you can focus on the actions for one milestone at a time, and will also allow you to realistically gauge the timescales of setting up your business.

---

### A moment to reflect

What are the main milestones on your roadmap? Do you need to raise funding, employ staff members, develop a product, or code some software? Can you run a 'skinny' business with minimal team and funding before growing? Think about how you see your business developing over the months and years, and the key milestones that you need to work towards along the way.

## *Example roadmaps*

As mentioned above, every roadmap is different, so perhaps the best way to demonstrate how a roadmap could look is to produce an example of how the tasks can be structured with a hypothetical business.

*Please note – this example doesn't include every possible task. The intention is to show how a roadmap might be put together. This example is deliberately less detailed in the stages, with consolidated tasks, as the key here is to focus on how the roadmap is prepared and structured, rather than the detail of the example. Don't worry; the important details are covered later in the book.*

### 'Super Administration Services'

In this example, the business owner has worked in an administration function for their whole working life and has decided that they would like to start their own business helping other small businesses access skills that they can't afford to have in-house. They want to employ one or two staff but to begin with they are happy to start on their own, helping people to manage their diaries, before employing a bookkeeper and a credit controller.

As the business can start with their own personal funds, the order of the stages will differ from a business requiring funding and a team.

#### Stage 1: Building client systems (deadline – end of month 1)

- Find a suitable CRM system, office suite, diary management system and IT hardware.
- Design forms for clients to use to book travel arrangements.
- Speak to five potential customers in a focus group.

Completion target – a third party can walk through the systems intelligently.

### Stage 2: Marketing and sales (deadline – end of month 1)

- Build a website, design a business card and stationery.
- Speak to directories.

Completion target – when all social media channels are set up, website is built and offline literature is prepared.

### Stage 3: Starting the business (deadline – end of month 3)

- Buy some initial stock of stationery.
- Find an office space.
- Phone 50 potential customers, meet with 10 prospects.

Completion target – two paying customers on a monthly retainer.

### Stage 4: Raising funds to go full-time (deadline – end of month 6)

- Get 10 paying clients on a monthly retainer.
- Prepare a formal business plan and financial projections.
- Get introductions to five bank managers and two private high net worth individuals.

Completion target – £30,000 financing, ideally by business loan.

### Stage 5: Increase services to cover bookkeeping (deadline – end of month 12 and £50k revenue)

- Find a bookkeeper to employ.
- Build a marketing plan.
- Find technology (recommended by staff member) to implement.

Completion target – two paying customers on a monthly retainer.

As you can imagine, the tasks and timescales become less specific as time goes on: there is little point detailing tasks at a granular level when there is uncertainty about the timescales and performance of previous stages.

We touched on the idea of project management earlier, insofar as understanding the milestones of the business. In the process of producing a roadmap, you will have found some areas that cannot be started until others are completed, and in other areas you will have noticed that they can run side by side with other projects. This issue is known as an issue of 'dependencies', and while I don't propose to go into any detail about project management for the purposes of these plans, I would suggest that you be aware of the notion that some activities rely on the completion of other activities and that you bear this in mind when producing your roadmap and adding activities to it.

Once you have put together the items in this chapter, you will have more than the average business plan! In the next chapter, we will look at what is needed for a 'formal' business plan; however, please don't disregard the work done so far. Some of it will fit into a formal business plan, yet the bigger purpose for this planning exercise is to give you a roadmap and a grounding from which you can operate the business successfully.

## Chapter 4 summary

In this chapter we have looked at how important it is to create a plan for yourself, rather than just for an investor or the bank. We've looked at both the traditional sections of a business plan, such as market research and competitor analysis, together with the broad concept of creating a business roadmap which will help you steer your business in the right direction.

Before proceeding to the next chapter, you should:

1   Think about all of the reflective questions within the chapter.

2   Download and review the Chapter 4 supplementary material from www.carlreader.com/bossit

3   Answer the following questions:

o   When will you commit to performing your market research? Please fix a date for starting and a date for completion and write down any actions that you may have that immediately come to mind.

o   When will you commit to performing your competitor analysis? Please fix a date for starting and a date for completion and write down any actions that you may have that immediately come to mind.

o   When will you pull together the remaining items and start producing your business roadmap?

_____
_____
_____
_____

# 05
# Raising funds

In this chapter you will:

- learn about the different types of funding available;
- understand the very real differences between debt and equity funding;
- take your planning activities and create a winning business plan;
- learn about how to create a realistic funding proposal;
- find out how to win over the bank manager!

Now that we've started the planning process, we should have a good understanding around the business – and not just the positives of the dream. One of the main benefits of taking a big picture idea and going through the steps in the previous chapter is that you are forced to critically appraise it, both against customer demands and your future competitors. Provided that this hasn't put you off forever, we're now at a point where we can consider the financial planning for the business.

It might be that you don't need funding. If you have enough savings available, you may be able to start the business with those – or perhaps, your spouse or partner may earn enough to cover household expenses while you start the business. Often, though, this isn't the case, and some assistance is needed to get the business off the ground.

You might find that you are fortunate enough to operate in an industry or location which has grants available for new businesses. Before diving into debt, you should certainly investigate these to see what is potentially available for your business. A note of caution, though – sometimes there is intense competition for these, and you might find that the steps required to achieve the grant are fairly onerous. Remember to take this into account when weighing up the best course of action for you and your business.

## A few words about debt

As mentioned in the section about Limiting Factors, I find that business owners' views and beliefs around business debt are shaped by their attitude to personal finances, and the words and phrases that they often heard growing up. For example, an entrepreneur who has historically juggled their personal finances and maxed out their credit cards may be more confident in their ability to service debt, while someone who considers a mortgage as their only debt may be far more prudent about borrowing for their business.

I cannot, and wouldn't want to, change anyone's personal paradigms. However, it is important to remember that phrases such as 'never a lender nor borrower be' *could* become limiting to the scope of a business – *if* debt-funding is the right way to structure the funding platform.

It might sound obvious, but there is a very real difference between 'good debt' and 'bad debt'. Clearly, bad debt would include debt that is not serviceable or is charged at a very high interest rate, but would also include debt that is incurred without need or objective justification. This would include consumer debt on credit cards, for luxury items. On the flip side, good debt is debt that allows you to invest and/or create an asset, and for the purposes of this chapter, the only debt that we will consider is this kind of good debt.

So, here is the nub of the issue. If you will need funding as a business owner, you will need to decide whether you want other people to lend you money as debt, with interest charged on it, or whether you would be happier to have people invest money in your business and take a share of the ownership and profits. As you can imagine, there are pros and cons for both options. For the purposes of this chapter, I would like you to forget the portrayal of funding on TV shows such as *Shark Tank* and *Dragon's Den*, and instead consider what is right for your business.

# Debt funding

Debt funding is the most common form of funding for small businesses from external parties.

## Small business loans and overdrafts

Debt funding is most commonly offered by banks, or other lending institutions, by way of a small business loan or an overdraft. Because of the nature of these institutions, funding arrangements tend to be rather rigidly structured, and the input that you can have in the process is limited. When seeking a loan from the major banks, it will often be an anonymous underwriting decision deciding whether or not you can have the money. This will be based on certain criteria such as affordability, interest cover, the security that can be offered and their lending criteria (which may be affected based on the industry that you are in or their current appetite to lend).

Outside of the main banks, debt funding is still available, but the debt is inherently considered to be riskier and, as such, the cost of the loan will be higher. With any business loan, you can expect to pay arrangement fees and interest, and there may possibly be certain conditions (known as covenants) that you would be expected to meet and report on.

Traditional bank loans and overdrafts aren't the only kind of debt funding available. Here are a few other options:

## Invoice financing

This is where a bank will either fund the value of your debtors (amounts owed to you by your customers), known as invoice discounting, or fund the value and manage the collection of these amounts, known as factoring. Both of these are useful financing options if you have to pay staff in advance of receiving cash from your customers; for example, if you are running a temporary staffing agency or a cleaning company. This method of finance can be more expensive than a loan and can be difficult to extract yourself from once it is up and running.

## Stock financing

Much as the name suggests, this is a method of financing that allows manufacturers and distributors to unlock the value of their stock and raw materials through the supply chain. It is often used in the automotive world, but could theoretically be used in any product-based business. For this type of funding, the lender would seek security through a charge over the stock, and would also keep the funding period to a set period of time (for example three months) to limit their risk of funding dead stock.

## Leasing

There are a number of types of leasing agreements available, but fundamentally they all allow businesses to acquire assets over a period of time. The main difference between the types of leases are that some offer ownership of the asset, whereas others are merely a rental, and the accounting treatment of both differs. Often, I would recommend that a business considers leasing as a way of spreading the risk for the lenders, so that no one lender is carrying all of the risk, which tends to be more appealing when a business needs to fund a large amount through debt funding.

### Peer-to-peer lending

Peer-to-peer lending has emerged as a valid source of 'alternative finance': in other words, an option other than the traditional banks. Put simply, peer-to-peer lending allows individuals to lend their money to businesses through a central funding company, who collect the individual finance amounts and then lend the money to businesses who apply. Something that you will need to bear in mind is that peer-to-peer lending is usually more expensive than bank funding. The investors are aware that it is a riskier 'asset' than savings, and the investors have times when their funds aren't used, yet still seek an annual return. Add the intermediaries' fees to this, and it is clear why the rates may be higher.

# Equity funding

When it comes to equity funding, there are probably even more options that need to be considered than with debt funding! Debt funding is relatively simple; once you have considered the cash flow impact of repayments and the total cost of the debt, you can compare different offers and types of funding with each other. With equity funding, on the other hand, the flexibility that can prove beneficial at the time of raising funds can also cause difficulties down the line.

Often, when we think of equity funding, we think of venture capital. This is usually limited to high-growth, high-return businesses – we've all heard the stories of multi-million-pound fund-raises, and the impact that this has on the traction of the business. The stories that we hear also tend to be focused on 'tech startups' rather than other businesses; however, equity funding is actually a possibility at all different levels and in all different types of industries.

At its simplest, an equity funding arrangement could involve two friends starting a business together, with one providing the 'IP' (intellectual property) of how to operate the business, and the other providing the funding to get the business started. Alternatively, it could be an arrangement between a parent and their adult child, with the child starting the business and the parent injecting funds to get it going in exchange for 25 per cent of the shares of the company.

These two arrangements are extremely common, and while they would not make the news in the way that a tech company achieving its latest funding round would, the matters to be considered are the same as those within a more 'venture capital' style arrangement. We'll cover venture capital in detail in Chapter 11.

# Equity or debt funding – which is right for your business?

Unfortunately, there is no 'one size fits all' answer about what would work better for you as a prospective business owner, as different types of funding suit different businesses. Typically, to be successful with venture capital backed equity funding, you would need a business with global ambitions, a scalable concept and a very large addressable market. This is due to how the venture capital market works, and the growth targets needed for the funds to make their returns. However, as we know, not all equity funding is venture capital backed, and it may be that a simple equity arrangement works well for both you and the investor. Debt funding also has its own limitations: financial institutions often look for security, and there is almost always a payback period built into the arrangement which requires positive cash flow to service.

**A moment to reflect**

While you might enjoy the 'win' of achieving equity funding, and
might not want to face any ingrained fears about taking on debt,
you need to put yourself in the shoes of your funders, and indeed
your business as a third party. What kind of funding is right for
you? Can you afford monthly debt repayments? Do you want to be
tied into having an investor until the day you sell the business?
Which is the lesser evil (or higher benefit, depending on what
they bring to the table) – a scary meeting with the bank manager
every year, or an external investor getting involved in your
business? Take a moment to think about what you want out of the
funding relationship, what would realistically be on offer, and
which route would best benefit the business.

Regardless of how you want to raise funds (debt or equity) and
regardless of who you borrow it from (a family member through to
a bank), it is *vital* that you make sure a strong agreement is in place
to protect all parties and to avoid any misunderstandings. For debt
finance, this would typically take the form of a 'loan agreement',
which would set out the term of the loan, the repayment schedule,
the amounts repayable, and the interest rate charged. For an equity
arrangement, this would agree the nature of the transaction, the
amount of shares transferred, and the rights attached to those
shares (such as the right to a financial return such as dividends,
voting rights, and the rights to the value of the shares if the business was to be sold). These agreements, known as shareholder
agreements, might also cover things such as the expectations of all
shareholders when it comes to input into the business or vesting
rights, and might also cover differences in the types of shares (for
example ordinary versus preference shares). Again, we will cover
the main considerations in Chapter 11 – but it will be very important for you to take independent legal advice on any agreement
that you enter into.

# Getting funding: writing a formal business plan

Now that you know the type of funding that you would like to achieve, it's time to put together the more formal business plan. You will recall that in the last chapter, I was very clear that the process of planning is very different from the process of putting together a business plan, and often the two tasks are combined and/or considered to be the same thing. For clarity, we're looking now at the document that your funders are expecting to receive, *not* the process that you need to go through to plan your business growth.

---

### Business plan vs pitch deck

If you're looking for debt finance, the bank will want a business plan, which would include some of the things that we discussed in the last chapter, together with financial projections. The equity investment world is a little different. For higher-growth businesses, the investors are looking more at product–market fit, the scale of the market and the founding entrepreneur and team. The initial document that they want to see is known as a pitch deck. The best way of differentiating a business plan and a pitch deck is that one is more structured, whereas the other is designed to 'sell' the concept and the high-level statistics. In any event, I would suggest producing a robust business plan, from which the key numbers and headlines can be extracted to include within a pitch deck.

---

A business plan is made up of two sections – words and numbers – and the elements included within the 'words' section were detailed in Chapter 4. For the numbers section, a bank will expect you to include the following:

Profit and loss projections – funders want to see projections for the period of the loan, showing an accounting profit and loss statement, broken down by month. Remember that this should be based on invoices, not cash, and will include accounting adjustments such as amortization.

Cash flow projections – from your profit and loss, you'll also be expected to produce cash flow projections for the period of the loan, to demonstrate affordability from a cash perspective. These will include adjustments to take into account the actual cash transactions. So for example, cash amounts would include sales taxes or VAT, and would also include debt finance received and repayments made. Each month would show whether the business has enough cash to service its commitments.

Balance sheet projections – unlike profit and loss statements, which demonstrate how a business has performed over a period of time, a balance sheet is a snapshot of what a business owns (its assets) versus what it owes (its liabilities), and how this is funded (its capital). The banks will look at the projected position of the balance sheet to understand the net assets and liquidity of the company, compared with the level of debt.

Typically, a bank manager would review these projections to ensure that the entrepreneur has been reasonable in their assessment of the marketplace and revenue, and also to check that the entrepreneur has included all potential costs of the business to a realistic level. If they are satisfied about this, they will then check the plans against their lending criteria, considering matters such as 'interest cover' (is there enough profit to cover the cost of lending?).

Depending on their desired outcome, an equity investor might look at these projections completely differently! For a fast-growth company, they might not actually want to see a profit in the first three years. This might seem nonsensical at first; however, businesses with an innovative idea and global potential are often in a race to acquire market share rather than profit, and investors might prefer them to reinvest any spare cash into marketing and product development. On the flip side, a family investor may take a similarly prudent view as a bank manager. The important step here is to understand what it is your investor is looking for – and before adjusting your plans to meet their views, ensure that it is the path that you would like to follow first.

## A moment to reflect

The outcome that your funders want might not necessarily be the outcome that you want. For example, venture capital (VC) companies are often mindful of the fact that a large proportion of their businesses will fail, and as such they only bank on those with the potential for explosive growth. If the pressure of this isn't what you envisaged when you embarked on this journey, that's absolutely fine – but be clear on it, and make sure that your views and those of your funders are aligned to avoid any conflict down the line.

It's clear that with different objectives, the definition of a 'winning plan' will be different from funder to funder. The best thing to do is to have an open and honest conversation in the early stages with your funder, to establish what it is that they are looking for within the plan and the business. This might save a lot of stress and heartache down the line.

Once you are clear on this, the preparation of the formal plan can get under way. I would recommend that you take professional advice on the plan to ensure that it is presented in the best possible way. An accountant should be able to help you produce the projections detailed above; however, it is important that you take ownership of the numbers and the key ratios within the projections. If you do decide to take professional advice, please ensure that you know exactly how the documents are made up, and what the numbers are based on! It would also be worthwhile getting the narrative of the plan reviewed by a few different people, to ensure that it is both understandable and compelling. What might seem obvious to you may not be to an outsider, and you need to ensure that the reader of your plan can understand what you do, how you do it, and why you do it as quickly as possible.

Then, it's simply a case of packaging and printing it! I would recommend that a business plan is around 15–30 pages maximum, and split roughly equally between words and numbers. Too little implies that no effort has gone into it, and too much appears daunting. You need to remember that the bank manager is a human too, and your job is to make your proposal as attractive as possible to them. No one enjoys trawling through reams of paper!

# The big day

Whether you're hoping to persuade a private individual to invest in equity in your business, or visiting the offices of a bank to ask for a loan, the preparation for the big day is the same:

**Make a great impression** – this should go without saying, but arrive on time, well prepared, and well presented. Banks don't necessarily expect you to wear your most formal outfit, but they do expect you to treat the occasion and their time with respect.

**Own your plan** – you need to be able to deliver your plan confidently. Make sure that you can present a compelling case about why they should fund you, as well as your business.

**Reinforce emotion with logic** – if you do a good job of presenting yourself and make a good first impression, you will need to back this up with logical reasons why they should invest in you. Knowing key data points about your industry and your business will help with this.

**Know your numbers** – we've all seen it on the business TV shows. A budding entrepreneur is tripped up by not knowing the difference between net profit and gross profit, or not understanding their margins. If these terms seem complicated, get an accountant to not only prepare your numbers, but to explain them fully until you understand them. It's a lesson that you'll need for raising funds and running a business.

**Don't just take the first offer** – it's rare that a bank will offer finance in the first meeting, but a private investor might. Regardless, if and when you receive an offer letter, make sure that you compare it against the market and any other offers that you may have, and make sure that you are comfortable with the terms. If you have any doubts or questions, now is the time to air them.

**Be prepared for the decision to be behind the scenes** – particularly with banks, you will find that the person that you meet isn't the person who will make the decision. It is unlikely that you will get the chance to even speak to the underwriter, let alone meet them. While the manager that you meet might be enthusiastic about your business, the underwriters might not be.

It's worth remembering that you might need to approach more than one bank or investor to get the funds to start your business, and you may need to continually adapt your plans as time goes on. A mistake that many business owners make is to approach their personal bank first, under the impression that this may help them in some way. In my experience, being an existing non-business customer of a bank holds little weight in their decision-making process, as the business departments are managed and staffed separately from the personal banking departments.

## A final note of caution

I cannot emphasize enough how important it is to have the right funder, and the right type of funding. Loans can be extremely rigid, overdrafts can be pulled away at any time, and factoring can be difficult to get out of. Equity investors might want to push the business beyond your comfort zone, and angel investors might be more interested in getting stuck in than you would like.

No form of funding is perfect, but you can make sure that the funding is right for you by creating a list of what you do and don't want from your business funders. Make sure that you shop around, consider all options, but then decide on what is right for *you*.

---

## Chapter 5 summary

In this chapter we have looked at the different types of funding typically available for your business. We have looked at the differences between debt and equity funding, both from a product perspective (how you receive the money and how the funder makes a return), and from a practical perspective of what the funder looks to achieve from the investment. We have run through the financial projections required to create a business plan, and have considered some of the practical things that you need to think about before meeting a funder.

Before proceeding to the next chapter, you should:

1  Think about all of the reflective questions within the chapter.

2  Download and review the Chapter 5 supplementary material from www.carlreader.com/bossit

3  Answer the following questions:

   o  What kinds of funding are appropriate for your proposed business?

   _____
   _____
   _____

   o  When will you commit to producing your financial projections and your final business plan? Make a note of any assistance you will need here, whether in the production of the documents or in the review stage.

   _____
   _____
   _____

o   When will you commit to meeting prospective lenders?

_____

_____

_____

# 06

# How to make the important first step

In this chapter you will:

- ensure that you have thought about some of the details behind starting a business;
- find a 'dream team' of advisers to help you on your way;
- learn how to select some of the key software tools that you will need;
- understand how to find your first customers and suppliers.

So we're coming towards the end of the planning process, but there are a few admin matters that we need to attend to before the business goes live. Some of these won't be relevant for you, but it is vital that you think about all of these before you dive head-first into running the business.

**Warning** – this chapter is going to be full of rapid-fire actions, so it might be worth putting together a to-do list!

## Choosing the right business type to trade with

Perhaps the first thing that you need to do when setting up any business is to consider how you are actually going to trade. In most countries, there are a range of different methods of trading, and they usually fall down to being 'incorporated' or 'unincorporated'.

The main difference between an incorporated and an unincorporated business is that an incorporated business is usually a separate legal entity from the individuals who run the business. An incorporated business usually requires some form of registration with the national and/or state registrar, and will require some level of paperwork to be completed before the business can start trading.

The advantage of a corporation is that the business can enter into contracts in its own right, can hold assets in its own right, and can incur debt in its own right. This offers a level of protection to the individuals starting the business, which is unavailable when trading as an unincorporated business. The downside is that the administration of setting up and managing an incorporated business is usually more costly and time-intensive.

Before deciding which type of business structure to use, you should do the following:

- Speak to a legal expert to understand the legal implications of each type of business format available to you.

- Speak to an accountant to understand any tax differences between the different types of businesses.

- Research your local government information to understand how to set the business up.

- Talk the decision through with any business partners to ensure that you are aligned on the decision.

We will cover the 'dream team' that you will need in your business later in this chapter, and this process shouldn't prove to be too costly.

## Register for taxes

No one enjoys the day that they have to pay their taxes, but it is a part of life that we can't avoid, and ethically it is something that we should do properly from day one. As part of the process of setting up the business, you should have found out the tax implications of the proposed business structure from your accountant.

One of the first things that you will need to do is to register your new business for any relevant taxes. This might include corporate taxes, payroll taxes and sales taxes such as VAT. Certain industries might require other registrations or declarations as well.

This is something that you can choose to do yourself, or you can outsource to an adviser for a relatively low cost. Given the fact that there are usually penalties for not handling your taxes correctly, it's worth taking external advice if you have any doubt about what you need to do to comply with your obligations.

# Prepare a partnership or shareholder agreement if needed

One of the first sayings that I heard in business was that 'a partnership is a sinking ship'.

That might not be true in your case – but let's be honest, no one ever goes into business with someone with the intention of it failing. The reality is that much like marriages, business partnerships can and do turn sour. There are several reasons for this, but in business they tend to come down to the fact that one side hasn't lived up to their end of the bargain.

If you are going into a partnership or a venture with someone else, have you and your potential business partners discussed what the bargain is?

The lack of clarity over mutual expectations is normally what causes these misunderstandings, which can develop into legal disputes.

While it may not be legally required, it is worth your time discussing an agreement between your partners, to ensure that you are all on the same page with how the business will operate. You can discuss things like ownership split, profit shares, who does what and how decisions are made. It's also a great time to cover the really tricky questions, such as what happens if the business doesn't succeed, and what happens if the partners fall out.

You don't necessarily need to take on a lawyer to do this, but personally I think it's a good idea; a business lawyer will have experience in preparing these documents, and perhaps more importantly, experience in defending them. They will spot things that you might not have thought of and will help provoke the difficult conversations. What's more, if the type of entity you are trading as requires this agreement to take a certain format, they can make sure it is prepared properly.

## Building the dream team

We've seen the need for some advisers so far in this chapter, and it might be sounding very expensive. Don't panic just yet!

The reality of running a business is that you can't do it all by yourself. None of us can rightfully claim to be experts in every specialism.

I have two types of support that I engage in my businesses – my 'dream team'; and external suppliers and advisers who I engage with on a professional basis. Sometimes members of my 'dream team' become suppliers, and vice versa. The 'dream team' is a group of friends in business, who help support each other and provide guidance in their own areas. My team includes marketing experts, sales experts, techies, legal experts, workplace culture experts… in fact, they cover pretty much every area of running a business. I like to think that I give back to them, too, but there are a couple of unspoken rules that we all adhere to: we only take what we give, and we don't take advantage of the situation!

When it comes to more formal advice, I would recommend every business finds a legal adviser and an accountant earlier than they think that they'll need them. The legal adviser can help ensure that the business is structured properly and that any agreements are robust; and the accountant can make sure that the business has done everything it needs to from a tax perspective and that the financial projections make sense.

# Work out the initial equipment that you need to buy

It's time to buy some new toys! Or maybe, not-so-new toys. You will have different equipment requirements depending on the type of business that you are running – some will need state-of-the-art tech, others will need equipment or tools. This is an area where new businesses can easily overrun on costs. Make sure that your purchases are all in line with your financial plans, and be strict with your budget.

One of the things that you will need to consider is whether you need to buy everything new, or whether you can source second-hand equipment. When balancing new vs second-hand, and indeed cheap vs expensive, make sure that you don't scrimp on the important things. There is no point buying something that will need replacing within a few months. I can tell you from personal experience, just last year, that a refurbished £150 computer was nowhere near enough for what I needed it for – its use was probably only for about three months, and they may well have been the least productive three months of my working life! It seemed like an ideal way to save some pennies at the time, but all I did was put off the inevitable of buying a modern system that could run all of the applications that I need, without any lag. Finding a balance between cost and performance is key.

# Find premises

Next up, you need to consider where you are going to run your business from! The kitchen table is great in the early days, but it can soon limit you. I've also found first-hand that there is a challenge juggling work and life, and if you can attempt to separate the two it will really help you focus on the business when you need to, and vice versa.

At the very least, you should try to find a devoted area in the house where you can work from. This would ideally be an internal or external room that can be used as an office. You may, however, decide from day one to use a serviced office, or if you are a premises-based business, you may decide to put an office area within your shop or factory. Serviced offices are great for the very smallest of businesses – while on the face of it they are more expensive, they allow you the flexibility to grow, and often the terms are much more flexible than a traditional lease. What's more, they take care of a number of the facilities such as light and heat and internet connections. They also will give you a community to work alongside – very important if you are starting out on your own.

## Set up phones

It might seem really old fashioned to some of you, and obvious to others, but you know what… some people will expect you to have a business phone line! If you live in a region that has similar numbers for mobile phones and landlines, such as the US, a mobile phone plan may suffice; however, in countries such as the UK that have devoted codes for mobile phones, you will probably want to consider either buying a landline phone or purchasing a geographical number for a VOIP/call diversion system.

Whichever route you go down, it is worth thinking about how you would like your customers to contact you. Do you want to get them to pick up the phone so that you can talk to them, or would you rather them fill in web forms or purchase online? Will your phone be used solely for customer service and reassurance, or for sales? Have a think about how your communication channels within your business will be used.

## Set up a website

More accurately at this stage, the first thing that you need to do is to secure the domain name for your business. Ideally this will be your trading name, but you might need to think of a creative variation on it.

Historically, businesses used to worry about exactly how their domain should be presented, and this worry was perhaps re-inforced when the 'top level' domains opened up. Marketers claimed that we'd all need a creative range of domains, and businesses panicked that their website would appear to be out of date. Search engine optimizers claimed that Google would rank the business based on its domain, so businesses panicked that they needed SEO-focused domains which include their keywords.

The reality of domain names today is that provided the website address is easy to read, easy to say (with no ambiguous spellings), and ideally is a .com site, you should be okay. Many of these names are taken so you might have to consider using hyphens, or a prefix such as 'team' as part of your domain name. These things are no-where near as bad as people feared just a few years ago. In an ideal world, your domain name will match your social media handles.

Once you have your domain name, which will also form part of your email address, you will need a website. This is an area where businesses can overspend both time and money. A website is of much less importance than it once was, and unless you are running a platform or e-commerce business online, you need to view the creation of the website as another task, not the most important task. A web designer will be able to help you create a site fairly easily, and it is important that you think of the mobile user experience first, given the trends of internet usage over the last decade.

## Set up a social media presence

Alongside your domain name is your social media presence. At this stage, I don't propose that you spend too much time on social media – in fact, this is a common area where business owners can creatively avoid the stuff they need to do. Instead, I would just suggest that you secure your username as a business page and/or an @handle on all major platforms, including Facebook, Twitter, Instagram, LinkedIn, TikTok and Snapchat. I would also suggest that you secure media sites such as Pinterest and YouTube.

While you may have no intention of using these platforms, it is important that you have as much ownership as possible over the names that you will be using for your online presence.

This is also a really good time to start thinking about the initial collateral that you will need to be promoting your business. You might already have a logo, but this won't necessarily be enough. Think about imagery that you can use, and perhaps any videos that you can create to help promote you and your business. We go into more detail about this in Part Three of the book.

## Set up an office suite and email

As you are at your computer setting up social media accounts, it's a good opportunity to set up some basic software that you will need in your business.

One of the first tools that you will need to rely on will be an office suite and an email program. My rule of thumb with most software now is to look at an online 'cloud' system first, and then only look at desktop versions if there is something you just can't do with a true online system – thankfully rarer these days. The online packages, such as Office 365 or Google Apps, are available for a monthly subscription, and it ensures that you always have up-to-date software, and that all data is automatically backed up.

You will also want to think about whether you need document storage, such as Dropbox, Google Drive or OneDrive, and a task management system.

## Choosing an accounting package

Similar to the above, you will need to set your business up on an accounting package to keep track of all of your transactions, and make sure that any tax filings are prepared on time. A decent package should also allow you to monitor your financial performance, so that you can compare your actual results with the plans that you made during your business planning process.

Ideally you should be looking at an online package that will connect with your bank account, through what is known as a 'bank feed', so that you don't have to manually enter all of your transactions into the system. These packages have a small monthly cost but should save you a significant amount of time. Your accountant might have a package that they recommend, but it is important that you are comfortable with the package too. There are a few market-leading software packages available globally, including QuickBooks, Xero and Sage.

## Choosing a CRM system

Another software package that you will need to consider is a CRM (customer relationship management) system. CRM systems now take many shapes and forms, and the type of system that you should use will depend a lot on the type of business that you are looking to run. For example, if you are setting up an e-commerce site, you might find that Shopify does everything that you need.

One of the most important changes in software packages over the last few years or so has been the move towards integrations, through the use of APIs (application programming interfaces). In simple terms, these allow different software packages to transfer data to each other. So, you can connect your CRM system with your accounting package and your email marketing software, to save you rekeying information into each. This is sometimes done through 'zaps' created in a package called Zapier.

On that basis, my recommendation is that you look for a CRM system (and indeed an accounting package, and any other software) that will 'play nicely' and transfer data seamlessly between each other, to minimize the amount of effort that you need to put into administration.

# Find your first suppliers

Every business needs suppliers of some sort, whether it is to provide stock to sell, or to provide ancillary services, so it's good to take some time thinking about how best to find and assess suppliers.

The internet is a wonderful thing, but it will lead you towards suppliers with a marketing budget! This can actually be a good sign, as it means that they are investing in themselves; however, it isn't necessarily a stamp of credibility. Make sure that your research goes beyond just a Google search, and that you look for real customer reviews. If you can, try to speak to existing customers to find out their experiences with the supplier – both from a product or service performance perspective, and about how the business works alongside them.

I would also suggest speaking to any trade associations that may be in your industry. Not only will they be a useful source of networking opportunities and education, but they will also help you find the reputable suppliers in your industry.

Whenever I'm considering a new supplier, I like to ask a few questions of myself to check that they are the right business for me:

- **Can the product or service be used today?** In other words, are they at the right point in their journey, and can they service my business appropriately?

- **Will the supplier be around in ten years' time?** Is their financial stability sufficient, so that I can be reassured that they will not go out of business?

- **Will the product or service be the same in ten years' time?** Or, are they likely to sell, merge, or pivot their business?

# Find your first customers

So, the final piece of advice I can give you at this stage is to find your very first customers! Daunting, but it needs to be done. We'll cover marketing in depth later in this book – in fact, Chapter 8 is devoted to it.

You might have had plenty of friends wish you well and tell you that they'd buy your product and service. Now is the time for them to put their money where their mouth is, as, quite frankly, you can't pay your bills with good wishes!

At this point, my recommendation is to get on the phone to everyone that you have been connected with, and let them know about your business. Make sure that you create a real buzz on social media about your new venture, and get people talking about it. If suitable, you might even want to think about hosting a launch party or an open day.

Find ways to try to hit the ground running, and remember the advice that I remember being given as a child:

*If you don't ask, you don't get.*

## Chapter 6 summary

In this chapter we have looked at some of the practical things that you will need to think about for your new business: from taking legal and financial advice to building a 'dream team' of advisers. We've looked at the kind of software that you may need in your business, some of the marketing tasks that you will need to kick off before starting and looked at the ways that you can appraise potential suppliers. We've also looked at the cold hard reality of buying equipment that you will need and working out where you are actually going to base your business. It has been a whistle-stop tour through a variety of areas, but these are the things that need sorting out pretty early on in your business journey.

Before proceeding to the next chapter, you should:

1   Think about all of the action points within the chapter.

2   Download and review the Chapter 6 supplementary material from www.carlreader.com/bossit

3   Answer the following questions:

o Within the supplementary material for this chapter is a checklist for you to make sure that you have addressed everything. When will you commit to downloading it and making sure that everything is in order?

_____

_____

o Your 'dream team' will really help you in business, both from a skills perspective but also from a support perspective. Have a think about some of the people who come to mind and make a note of them. What can they bring to the table? Is there anything you can offer them – such as reciprocal advice, or even the offer of being part of a mutual support network?

_____

_____

_____

_____

o Perhaps the hardest thing here is getting on with the 'ask' in the final section and starting to make some sales calls. It is far too easy to dive head first into a social media campaign with no strategy – it's much tougher to actually speak to people and let them know what you are doing. Why not commit to a day of activity now? Note down the day that you will commit to doing this and clear your diary. It might be your most productive day in business so far...!

_____

_____

# Part Three
# Do it

# 07

# Building your systems and processes

In this chapter you will:

- take stock of what you have achieved to date;
- learn about the importance of using strong processes and systems to run your business;
- find out the different ways to develop and document your processes;
- understand what makes a process effective and efficient.

**F**antastic news! At this point in the journey, you have done most of the hard work. You've created the business idea, worked out whether there is a market fit and produced a whole bunch of plans and documents about how it could all work out. You've started the business, registered everything that needs registering, opened a bank account and made your first sale. Life is good...?

At this point in the journey, it can be tempting to put your foot down on the gas and try to grow as quickly as possible.

After all, you don't have the security of a monthly pay cheque anymore and you may feel that there's nothing to lose.

How can more customers *hurt* my business?

How could getting more cash in the bank be a *bad* thing?

Why *shouldn't* I grow my business?

Some of my advice in this chapter might seem like a contradiction, as I often say that action – the 'do' part of the process – is where most business owners get it wrong. Why would I suggest that business owners do anything that doesn't equate to direct action towards their dream?

The thing is, there's a difference between working *smart* and working *hard*. There are different types of action. And when running a business, decisions are rarely binary.

# Walking before you run: why systems and processes are important

First things first, let's have a think about the theory behind why you should perhaps take things a little slower than you might wish to.

When running a business, you are often juggling various tasks. Most of us know this, but we tend to think of the tasks as customer-facing tasks. The balls that we have in the air are customer emails, sending out proposals, designing new marketing material and actually doing the stuff that we are paid for.

The problem is, these are only some of the balls that we're juggling. They are the obvious ones, and the urgent ones. They are the tasks that we need to do to get new customers, do our work and get paid. If we drop one of these balls, we know about it pretty quickly.

If we put our foot down on the gas, as suggested earlier, there's one big problem. More balls to juggle! Emails get missed, calls get diverted to voicemail and customers get let down. We forget to pay suppliers, which means that products or services are withheld. We neglect our business finances, so end up spending more on marketing than we really can afford to. All in all, the balls end up crashing on the floor at some point.

It's also worth considering how things look from a customer's perspective. Would you be happy to find out about a product or a service, and then having the supplier work out how to sell it to you, and then how to deliver? While you might intuitively know how to convert a sale and deliver on your promises, it isn't very scalable.

If you decide to grow your business, you will need processes that future team members can follow and be held accountable to.

Otherwise, you will be left juggling those balls yourself. And we know what that can lead to!

To avoid ending up with balls all over the floor, it's vital that we make our job of juggling the various tasks in our business a little easier. This is where processes and systems come in.

---

### A moment to reflect

Let's take our juggling analogy a little further: of the balls we juggle, some are rubber balls and some are crystal balls. The rubber balls can be dropped, and will be perfectly reusable once they're dusted off – but the crystal balls may smash at any point. By introducing the non-urgent 'rubber balls' such as process mapping now, you can help prevent smashing the 'crystal balls' of important customers and cash in the bank.

Perhaps most importantly, we need to remember that the crystal balls include our health, family life and wellbeing. As business owners, we can have a tendency to neglect these areas of our lives – particularly in the early days of the business. Part of the reason that we use systems and processes to help us is so that we don't break these precious crystal balls.

---

## What are systems and processes and how are they different?

Before marching on and discussing how we can go about setting up systems and processes to help us juggle effectively, it's worth looking at just what they actually are. Often, the words are used interchangeably by business owners, but this isn't quite accurate:

System – a system brings together a group of *processes* within a certain area of a business.

**Process** – a process is a sequence of tasks or events (known as *procedures*) that enable a defined outcome to happen.

**Procedure** – a procedure is one step of a *process*, and the completion of each procedure should be required to properly complete an efficient process.

**Instruction** – an instruction is a guide for team members to be able to complete the procedures within a process and use various processes to achieve the results required for the system.

---

**Important:** These terms are often colloquially used interchangeably (eg 'you didn't follow the system' rather than process). Also, please bear in mind that a 'system' can also refer to a tool used within a procedure – such as a software package. This can be confusing, so for the purposes of this book, we will stick to the definitions here.

---

## Systems

Let's start from the big picture and get smaller. Before designing processes for certain parts of your business, it is worth taking a step back and mapping out the areas in which you need systems. This will help you design processes to sit within those systems, which can then help you identify the procedures needed to make the processes work.

For most businesses, these are the first areas that you should consider:

- lead generation (marketing);
- lead conversion (sales);
- doing the work (operations);
- staff recruitment and management (human resources);
- managing money (financials).

If you've thought about the above list while reading it, you might have noticed that I have deliberately omitted customer service. Some businesses aim to design separate customer service processes, but I prefer to include customer service as the ultimate outcome of each process and system within a business. However, like my approach to customer service systems, if you decide to omit a key area from your system planning, do make sure that area of your business is covered adequately.

---

### A moment to reflect

Now is an ideal time to reflect on what it is that you want from your business. We discussed earlier in the book about different personality types: the work that we are discussing in this chapter sits firmly within the 'managerial' side of our roles as entrepreneurs. If you can't think of anything worse than documenting systems and processes, it is an ideal time to reflect on whether you'd be happier as a self-employed individual, as this kind of work will consume your time during the early stages of scaling a business. Alternatively, if you have sufficient funding, you can aim to recruit operational managers in the early days; however, they are often an overhead that startup businesses struggle to afford.

---

## Measuring systems

Once you have identified the areas that need systems, you should think about what the desired outcome for the system is, and the metric you will use to measure it. What single number or statistic would help you know whether or not that part of the business is working? For marketing, it may be the value of your pipeline, or the number of leads generated. A sales system should really focus on the value of orders, but is that really important if the orders aren't profitable? These results that should be tracked are known as KPIs (key performance indicators).

The problem with KPIs is that they can sometimes be conflict-ing, as in the sales example above. So, once we start, we have a natural human tendency to include more and more KPIs within our systems – leading to the really important stuff being missed.

I have some very simple methods that I use to try to keep focus on what is important in my businesses:

1 For the financials, identify the three biggest numbers in the profit and loss account – for most businesses, this is made up of revenue (total income), gross profit (total income less costs directly related to the income, such as product purchases), and total overheads (every cost that cannot be directly allocated to the income).

2 For my staff, I focus on staff engagement scores via independent surveys, staff churn (what percentage of staff members do we replace over the year) and performance results.

3 For operations, it varies depending on the type of business, but typically I would be looking at throughput (how quickly a job or product moves through the system), customer satisfaction through simple surveys or using a net promoter score, and failure rates (number of mistakes made or value of faulty products).

4 For sales, it ultimately comes down to the contribution that sales make to the profitability of the business. So, revenue and profitability per sale is something that I'd keep a keen eye on, but underneath these headline statistics I'd also be looking for more detailed stats such as sales conversion rates based on the type of sale and sales value per staff member/square foot of a premises.

5 For marketing, I find it much trickier, as there isn't always a direct return that can be tracked to an activity. So instead, I like to ensure that marketing spend is on track to budget, and monitor the value of the pipeline. I also keep an eye on the split of lead sources, to ensure that processes and activities tie in to where income is actually coming from.

You can probably see that the above suggestions are fairly generic, and can be implemented with little changes into most types of business. It is still important to check that the KPIs that are designed actually meet what you want to achieve from each function, and that you have an adequate balance when KPIs potentially conflict with each other.

# Processes

We've now identified what systems we need, and the results that we want to achieve in each area. The way that we make a system work, though, is by putting effective and efficient processes in place. As alluded to earlier, in the early days, most processes are already in place – albeit only in the mind of the entrepreneur. To make a business truly scalable, a business owner needs to take all this intellectual property that is sitting in their head and get it down into a process that others can follow.

A great process ticks the following boxes:

**Effectiveness** – the process directly impacts a KPI that the system's success depends on.

**Efficiency** – the process has no superfluous steps, and thought has been given towards minimizing friction between the procedures, reducing the overall time spent on the process.

**Completeness** – likely 'what if' scenarios have been covered and included within the process as optional steps, reducing the number of deviations from the system.

**Clarity** – the process is easily understood from a procedural level, but perhaps more importantly the need for both the process and the system can be understood by anyone who follows the process.

I mentioned earlier in this chapter that I prefer processes to have as much customer service focus as possible. In the absence of a 'customer service system', I like to put myself in the shoes of both the customer and the team member to sanity-check any process, and make sure that it results in a positive outcome for both sides.

You should also remember that a process is never completed – technology changes, and this is what tends to have the biggest impact on a procedural level. Also, we are all human, and it is very rare for our first attempt at a process to meet all of the four criteria listed above. In the early stages of a business, we need to remember that we are simply looking to document the processes, not necessarily to build them to a corporate standard.

## *Documenting a process*

There are a number of ways of documenting a process, ranging from the bare minimum through to over-complication. A process could simply be a 'to do' list of three procedures on a scrap of paper, or it could form part of a business management software package with various dependencies and other complications.

Often, for a new business, the ideal system can be mapped out as either a checklist or a flowchart. For the simplest of processes, I tend to prefer a checklist, as it forces the document to be easily understood and simple to use. A flowchart can help you visualize the entirety of the process as the business develops, including the various different process flows that should happen when there is a deviation from standard. There are software packages available to help build both, such as LucidChart, draw.io, and even Microsoft Excel (my software of choice for simple one-off documents).

It is really important not to over-complicate, or over-think, the processes in your business. While we can get carried away with trying to plan for every possible permutation, sometimes it is worth just building a 'version 1' process to make sure that the important procedures happen. A process can be developed over time, just as everything else in your business will develop.

Table 7.1 provides an example of a simple checklist-style process.

**Table 7.1** Process checklist

| Process: Respond to a customer support request | Completed |
|---|---|
| 1 – Acknowledge receipt of the support request personally, with your contact details and expected time of response, following the automated response by email using the templated response. | |
| 2 – Log the support request in the CRM system and allocate the task to yourself. | |
| 3 – Check our internal 'wiki' to see if this matter has a templated response. | |
| 4 – If there are any unexpected delays to the response time, inform the customer as early as possible and ask if there are any ways that you can help in the meantime. | |
| 5 – Respond to the support query, ensuring that you provide telephone contact details in case of any difficulties. | |
| 6 – Log the response in the CRM system and mark the task as 'responded'. | |
| 7 – Diarize to contact the customer after 24 hours and check that the issue has been resolved, with reference to both the issue and the customer's circumstances to keep the communication personal. | |
| 8 – Log the response in the CRM system and mark the task as 'completed'. | |
| 9 – If there was no templated response in step 3, please create a 'wiki' entry for this support enquiry and ensure that it is tagged correctly so that others can search for it. | |

This is one way a simple process could look within the operations of a business. One thing that you would notice if you read through it carefully is that the individual procedures rely on technology such as CRM systems and emails, and a large proportion of this process could actually be automated by using a customer ticketing system such as ZenDesk, LiveAgent or FreshDesk. When processes are mapped out like this, one benefit is that efficiencies like opportunities to use software solutions become really clear; however, it is important to balance the time you spend researching new solutions to improve efficiency with the work that you need to do to build your business.

Whichever route you choose to proceed, the most important thing is to ensure that the process is both complete and logically ordered, and easily understood.

## Operations manual

The preparation of a process is a great theoretical exercise in checking what you do on a day-to-day basis in your business, but let's be honest – we are only doing this to improve our business and make it easier to juggle the balls. Even the best process won't improve our business if it isn't followed.

Earlier, we highlighted 'clarity' as a key part of making a process work for you and your team. Without each procedure being clearly and concisely defined, it is very difficult to expect the process to be followed. The challenge with concisely defining a process – by nature, something of an overview – is that it's difficult to include any level of instruction about how to perform the task without making the whole process unwieldy. This is where an operations manual can come in – to help tie together all of the systems, processes and procedures in a business.

Often used in franchises, an operations manual is the 'bible' of a business. It pulls together everything that the business should depend on, from opening the doors through to cleaning up in the evening. It is here that you should expect your systems to be collated, your processes documented and your procedures explained. You would expect to include the 'instruction manual' for common tasks on software applications; and anything else for a new employee to be able to pick up the manual and run the business.

When we think of operations manuals, we often think of dusty old books that are never actually used. Nowadays, these manuals tend to be dynamic documents online, and can take the form of a wiki or an intranet. When building one, it is important to think of it as a 'loose leaf folder' rather than a hardback book – an operations manual should always be a work in progress.

## A moment to reflect

In this chapter we have covered a lot of theory, and it may seem very daunting in the early days of running a business. You might feel comfortable running your business without formal processes and manuals at this stage, which is absolutely fine – at this stage, all I ask is that you understand what constitutes an effective system, process and procedure; that you are aware of the need to document them as the business grows; and change them as circumstances change.

## Chapter 7 summary

In this chapter we have looked at how important it is to think about systems, processes and procedures in your business. We've looked at the difference between them, and identified the areas in which systems are needed in your business. We considered what are the key attributes of a great process, and explored how to develop a process that is actually used and understood. We've also thought about why this is important.

Before proceeding to the next chapter, you should:

1  Think about all of the reflective questions within the chapter.

2  Download and review the Chapter 7 supplementary material from www.carlreader.com/bossit

3  Answer the following questions:

o  When will you commit to thinking about systems, processes and procedures? While they don't necessarily need to be produced yet, think about the areas in your business where you will need systems, and when the right time would be to produce the processes. Try to map out just one process to get the ball rolling.

_____

_____

_____

_____

o  What areas of your business need systems?

_____

_____

_____

o  What process will you attempt to create as part of this exercise?

_____

_____

_____

_____

# 08
# Finding your customers and marketing

In this chapter you will:

- understand what makes a customer want to buy from you;
- learn about the different methods of finding customers;
- learn some basic marketing and sales principles;
- find out how to build a basic marketing plan.

In any business, there are two core activities – finding customers and keeping customers – which ultimately dictate the success or failure of the venture. Without a steady and predictable flow of customers, you will be left unable to make any strategic decisions and could quite easily fall into the trap of many 'lumpy businesses' (named after the nature of their cash flow), living on a 'famine-or-feast' basis.

Likewise, if you can't keep customers, you will also have a very difficult time. Generally speaking, it is more expensive to find new customers than to retain existing customers, who already have some form of loyalty to you. Also, people talk! If your offering is not at the right standard for a second or third purchase, others will hear about it. Imagine being on the business treadmill – failing to keep customers is like increasing both the speed and the incline at the same time.

We've already covered some of what you need to know about helping you with these activities in the last chapter. The theory behind processes and systems can help you design ways to make it easier for your business to find customers and keep customers. In this chapter, we will be taking a helicopter view of the worlds of marketing and finding customers – and in Chapter 9, we will round this off by looking at how you can keep these customers, and make sure that your business continues to run profitably and successfully.

---

### A moment to reflect

Many business owners believe that if they have the 'magic bullet', work will come to them. That a great website will attract web traffic. A great location will attract high footfall in store. The best product will fly off the shelves. A great service for one client will attract scores of similar clients. This simply isn't true. Rather than 'aggressively waiting for the phone to ring', this chapter will help you decide how best to promote and grow your business.

---

## Designing your ideal customer avatar

Before diving into any marketing activities, it is worth thinking about what your ideal customer looks like: who is it that you want your business to be serving?

There is no single way to design this, but I find that asking a range of questions – such as those below – helps me to get under the skin of my ideal customer and work out what it is that they want:

- How old are they?
- What kind of work do they do?
- What are their goals in life?
- Do they prioritize health, family or career?
- Do they prefer low-cost or premium products?

- As a child, how would they have behaved?
- What kind of books do they read?
- What films do they watch?
- Who would be their first and second choice of political parties?
- What issue is most important for them?
- Where would they spend their free time?
- What would be the three main things that they look for in their lawyers?
- Do they use lots of make-up and cosmetics?
- Which social media site would they use?
- What kind of shops would you see them buying from; and where would they go window shopping?
- What websites would they visit frequently?
- What kind of car do they drive? Model? Electric or fossil fuel?
- How would they dress for their best friend's wedding? For their neighbour's wedding? For a loose acquaintance's wedding?
- Would they rather build a shed or have it delivered and installed?
- Who do they bank with?
- If they bought a luxury product, would it be straight on Instagram or 'saved for best'?

You can see that this is a really eclectic mix of questions, to give you an idea of the kind of questions that you should be asking yourself. Rather than just listing a set of demographic data, this exercise really helps you think about why your customer does what they do, the kind of messages that they would be receptive to and how to reach them. Please bear in mind that this list isn't definitive, nor prescriptive. Feel free to design your own questions – but try to be as wide-ranging as possible. The trap that some business owners fall into is that they only ask 'blinkered' questions – for example, an accountant might only ask questions around how someone buys accounting services. It is the breadth of questions across all sorts of matters that helps you really understand the motivations of your customer.

Once you understand who your ideal customer is, you are then able to design marketing collateral and a customer service process that meets or exceeds their expectations.

# Should I pick a niche market for my business?

Particularly in professional B2B (business-to-business) services, a question that is often asked is whether a business should focus on a 'niche' market rather than the general market. The argument against having a 'niche' is that it may result in needing to turn away customers that don't fit the target market.

Taking a step away from that rather narrow question and type of business, I'd first comment that every business has a target market of some sort, whether it is described as a 'niche' market or not. Waitrose knows exactly who their customers are, as do Boots, Mercedes and Poundland. From that definition, they are able to adapt both their marketing and their customer service to meet their customers' expectations, as mentioned earlier. However, it doesn't stop them from providing their products and services to other paying customers! A high net worth individual should get exactly the same product and customer service in Poundland as anyone else, despite the marketing not being targeted at them.

From that perspective, knowing that you're not prevented from dealing with people outside of your target market should reassure you that you won't be turning people away at the door. Now, we can consider the benefits of being clear on what your ideal customer looks like:

- You can target your messaging so that it appeals to their personal value set.

- You can demonstrate how your product or service can help them reach their goals.

- You can promote yourself on the websites that they browse and in the magazines that they read.

- You can use the music genres that they are keen on and introduce the cultural references that they'll understand.

- You can have a face-to-face or telephone conversation with them at their level.

- Ultimately, you will know what they want to buy and how they like to buy it.

I'm yet to be persuaded that this isn't a good thing!

# What are the different ways of promoting my business?

Anyone who has been in any sort of business development role will know that there are countless ways of promoting a business – and while every solution is promoted as a magic pill, those of us who have been in business for some time know that there is a rule of thumb that says only about half of a business's marketing spend works. If only we knew which half!

## Direct and indirect marketing

Before looking at the specific activities that you can do, it is important that we distinguish between two different types of marketing: direct and indirect.

Direct marketing: this is the stuff that has a direct impact on the sales of a business, or perhaps more accurately, that can be fully tracked and measured to a specific prospect action. Examples of direct marketing could include payments to referral partners, pay-per-click advertising and direct mail campaigns.

Indirect marketing: this covers things that are needed for a business to appear credible in the marketplace, but don't necessarily lead to any sales. They do, however, support the direct marketing activities undertaken. Examples of these would be logo design, printed literature and signage.

This is a very broad way to distinguish activities, but it's a useful sanity check for any business owner to monitor the amount of direct and indirect marketing that they undertake. If either type of activity is not covered, it is likely to make the other ineffective. For example, a business that focuses solely on direct marketing might be deemed to lack substance; conversely, a business that focuses solely on indirect marketing might have amazing marketing collateral that no one actually sees. By working on a careful balance in both areas, businesses can improve the conversion rates of their direct marketing, which should ultimately lead to more sales.

It's also wise to remember that indirect marketing can still be measured to some extent. Websites can be reviewed for statistics such as bounce rate, click-through rates and average visitor duration. Focus groups can help you gauge how well a brochure or logo resonates with your customers. Just because you can't track an amount of payment to a specific customer, it doesn't mean that you should leave the activities unmeasured.

## *Marketing activities*

Now that we know a broad way of splitting marketing activities, it's time to look at some of the different activities that a business can undertake:

### Organic online marketing

In today's world, many businesses naturally gravitate towards this type of activity; however, without supporting activities, it is very difficult to actually generate leads by using online marketing alone. Activities include building a website, participating in industry forums and producing content (covered in more detail below).

More specifically to this category, here we would also include search engine optimization (SEO). In the mid-2000s, this was a large spend for businesses trying to increase their prominence on search engines like Google, and there were a number of ways of optimizing websites to ensure that your website appeared on page one of the keywords where you wanted to be found. This was achieved by ensuring that a page appeared relevant to Google's algorithms, but was sometimes open to abuse by 'black hat' (hacking) methods. Nowadays, Google's algorithms have evolved to a point where they can more intelligently identify the relevance of a site. Over the last decade, they have also covered areas such as location, mobile-friendly websites, and web user experience to ensure that organic search results are the best that they can provide. With this, the role of an SEO expert has evolved from copywriting and adapting a site's content to that of a 'housekeeper' ensuring that the entire user experience is at the level it needs to be.

## Paid search marketing

It's no secret that if you want to be number one on Google, the only sure-fire way is to pay for the position. Google uses a method called 'pay per click', where businesses can bid for the position, based on a payment per user that clicks through to their website. While this appears to be a 'no brainer', as it is a direct marketing activity, there are a number of things to consider.

The most obvious issue is the actual cost per click. At its simplest, if you overpay per click you won't have a profitable business. Each click brings a website visitor, so you need to calculate the cost per converted customer, using the conversion rates at each point in a prospective customer's journey.

You also need to think about how you can reduce the cost per click that Google charges you. Despite how it may seem at first, the 'winner' of a pay-per-click bidding auction might not pay the most for the clicks. Google can reward and penalize websites on factors such as relevance and site quality.

## Organic social media marketing

Following organic web marketing, this is probably the second area that businesses identify as something to focus on, but again without standout content or creativity, it can suffer the same fate as general web marketing. For all intents and purposes, and given today's consumer expectations, social media marketing is now intrinsically linked with general internet marketing.

For those looking to build a social media presence, it's important to remember two things:

- Business is no longer B2B or B2C, it's H2H – human-to-human – because people buy from people.
- Metrics are irrelevant if they don't lead to money in the bank.

When building a social media campaign, you should focus on personality rather than a corporate sales pitch, even if you will be 'Tweeting' or 'Instagramming' from a corporate account. Companies like Tesco and Specsavers are great examples of how a personal tone can be combined with a set of corporate brand guidelines.

You also need to build your profile where your customers are, and create content that is in line with the platform. One of the best tips that I've ever been given about social media is that it's important to listen first, and learn the culture! Every platform is different, and what works on TikTok might not work on LinkedIn.

## Paid social media marketing

Growing an organic social media following is a tough, and often thankless, task. Thankfully, in a similar way to Google search results, you can increase your visibility through paid social media marketing.

Every site operates slightly differently, but broadly you can pay for clicks (similar to Google) or for impressions (views on a user's page). Much like Google, these are competitive marketplaces and you need to make sure that you are paying an appropriate amount per view/click to stay profitable. One of the key benefits of paid social media campaigns is that you can refine your audience, based on demographics and interests.

The power of this is far greater than many imagine. Think about what would be more effective – a generic TV advertisement for a beer company costing £1 million, or 1 million bespoke adverts costing £1 each, tailored to the interests and hobbies of each user.

It's clear that while the social media campaign would require far more investment and management, the conversion would be significantly greater.

Much like organic social media marketing, you also need to consider the user behaviour on each site. Users of Instagram, for example, might be far more inclined to make a product purchase than users of Reddit. Again, a great way of starting to understand what would work for your business is simply to look at what shows up in your news feeds across the various platforms, and consider what works for you.

## Influencer marketing

An evolving strategy, influencer marketing involves providing social media influencers with products and/or payments in exchange for them promoting a product or service on their social media feed.

Already there has been some level of controversy around this method of marketing, with influencers not clearly indicating that a promotion is paid for by using the #ad hashtag, and with some influencers having fake followers to artificially inflate their reach.

While the likes of Kim Kardashian might be out of the reach of most businesses, and it's important to be careful in this arena, I believe that there is still a place for 'micro influencers' in your field to help you promote your product or service. Before engaging an influencer, it is important to be clear on what you are hoping to achieve from a campaign, and what constitutes success. Social media platforms are notoriously fickle, and it is near impossible to predict the success or otherwise of an individual post. What does remain within your control is the type of post, number of posts and the messaging around them.

Another note of caution is that I would advise all businesses to find influencers that are a natural advocate of what you do – the ideal influencer being an existing customer. There is nothing more off-putting to a potential customer than the incongruence of a serial influencer advertising protein shakes on Monday and piles of chocolate on Tuesday.

## Online advertising

The last of the solely online channels that we will consider, online advertising, is a declining area of spend for many businesses, but is still worth considering from a brand awareness perspective. In the early days of the internet, banner adverts were extremely popular, but as users became accustomed to them, a phenomenon known as 'banner blindness' came into play, and users didn't acknowledge their presence on a page.

That said, there are still opportunities for online advertising to work for your business, particularly if it is approached intelligently. Most online portals (such as news sites) are sustained by advertising, and provided that the advertising is relevant and beneficial to both the content and the user experience, a campaign can prove to be a success.

Email marketing is another form of online advertising, as a natural evolution of direct mail. Following a global shift towards data protection and an improvement in the filtering of email applications, the value of email marketing has reduced somewhat, but there is still a value in holding a legitimate database and performing regular email promotions.

## Offline advertising

With the plethora of online options available, offline marketing is often forgotten, and advertising is one of the pillars of offline marketing that it would be a mistake to overlook. Advertising in local, national or trade press helps provide a level of credibility and brand awareness that an online campaign can struggle to match.

The challenge with offline advertising is that it is notoriously difficult to track. Magazine adverts might be seen by people in doctors' surgeries and airport lounges, as well as those who purchased the magazine. Not only is it hard to pin down the number of viewers, it isn't normally very targeted, as you can't refine your audience in the same way that you can with paid social media marketing.

There is a growing trend for publishers to offer content marketing opportunities alongside adverts. While this might seem like you have free rein to create two adverts, you should always be mindful of the reader's experience and ensure that you make the most of the opportunity to demonstrate expertise, rather than a sales pitch.

## Content marketing

A particular favourite of mine, content marketing is a great way to build credibility in what you offer and how you do it. At its heart, content marketing is creating valuable information in all its forms, for users to learn something that they didn't know before. This can include blog posts, infographics, social media updates, columns in magazines and videos.

One of the big concerns that business owners have about embarking on a content creation campaign is that they are afraid of giving away all of their intellectual property. For me, this myth is unfounded, as if you search hard enough the information is probably out there anyway – and if someone isn't prepared to pay you for what you actually do, they aren't a customer worth having.

Another problem that I see with many business owners embarking on a content creation campaign is that they suffer from 'creative avoidance', doing anything that they can to avoid getting on with creating great content. This tends to particularly manifest itself in searching for the latest and greatest tools and equipment! To produce better quality content than 99 per cent of businesses, all that is needed is a smartphone, a computer, a lapel mic and a tripod. And something worth sharing! We'll go into more detail about how to create a content plan later in this chapter.

## PR

Many new businesses worry about embarking on a PR campaign, as they're worried that PR can be expensive and difficult to track – both very valid concerns, particularly if it is approached from a vanity perspective rather than with a strategic aim. On the flip side, though, it can be a great way of building credibility in your marketplace and can provide great bang for your buck if approached cleverly.

I have personally done a lot of PR for my businesses, and can count on one hand the number of press releases that my team or I have sent. Instead, we tend to look at the activities that we can do that would pique a journalist's interest, and ensure that we are in the right place at the right time. The business world is full of some amazing examples of businesses that have embraced PR effectively to tell their story, and perhaps one of the best campaigns of recent years has been the Dove Campaign for Real Beauty, which tied in their traditional advertising with a concerted PR effort to spread their message.

As a startup business, you won't have the budget of a corporate like Dove to engage the world's biggest agencies, but you will be able to do stuff that gets you noticed by journalists. Low-cost activities that will put you on the radar of the press include responding to #JournoRequest posts on Twitter, attending 'Meet The Journalist' events and networking at events where the press are likely to be. With a clear story about why you are different – which, most importantly, has to be interesting to a third party rather than you – you will be surprised at how far speed of response, courtesy and relationships can take you.

## Personal branding

Linked to PR somewhat is the power of personal branding. In today's world, we live in a sadly automated society. We are social beings at heart, but are dealing with other people less and less in our day-to-day lives. We now live in the 'stay at home economy' – using Uber Eats rather than visiting restaurants, watching Netflix rather than going to the cinema, and generally not having the same amount of human contact that we would have done even just five years ago.

While businesses have had a concerted push towards systemization over the last couple of decades, the brands that stand out nowadays are those that embrace the perfectly imperfect human nature of their team, and who provide a great service with a human face. We touched on this earlier in this chapter in the social media section, and referred to business now being H2H (human-to-human).

## Networking

Networking is a marketing exercise that can either energize you or fill you with dread! I've yet to come across a more polarizing method of promoting a business than networking, and while I enjoy networking with others, I also fully empathize with those who'd rather not spend their time in a room full of people they don't know, making small talk. While I could use the limited space in this section attempting to persuade you of the benefits of networking and creating powerful connections, I'm realistic enough to appreciate that some readers will simply not want to attend these events.

On that basis, I'd like instead to focus on what I believe is the main thing to remember when starting networking. Perhaps the biggest realization for me was when I truly understood that networking wasn't about selling to the attendees – instead, every networking event was simply an opportunity for me to meet some more people, and get to know them personally. Effective networking results in strong connections over time, and once they begin to know, like and trust you, they will naturally want to help you out by becoming an advocate and supporter of your business. Rather than tracking how many sales conversations that you have at a networking event, focus on having a number of meaningful conversations and connections. After all – no one goes to a networking event to be sold to!

## Client and prospect entertaining

Once you have some customers on board, you might want to think about arranging events so that they can meet each other, meet your new prospects and enjoy the hospitality that you can offer. If you're going to go down this route, you'll want to invite a good mix of both clients and prospects, as it allows your existing clients to offer 'social proof' from someone who has already purchased your products or services.

Perhaps the biggest problem with this is that there is a minimum investment to make it worthwhile. To make the event sufficiently attractive for people to travel and attend, it needs to be either a sporting event or a high-level dinner, and to make it worth your time you will need a reasonable number of attendees. Provided that your customers are of sufficient value, however, you may well find that it offers great value for money as it affords you the opportunity to spend quality time with key customers and prospects.

## Telemarketing and direct mail

Finally, I've combined two 'old school' methods of marketing – telemarketing and direct mail – and I don't believe that I need to explain what they are to you, as we've all had those phone calls and mass-mailed leaflets! Many people have strong opinions about receiving unsolicited phone calls, or 'junk mail' through their door, and these are methods that are undoubtedly on the wane.

What I would say, though, is that you shouldn't write off any marketing method just because it seems outdated or because you don't like being the recipient personally. In my own business, a direct mail campaign proved to be the most successful campaign that we ran in a decade; it generated millions of pounds in revenue, simply because it was performed in 2008, at the time that every other business was cutting mail budgets and focusing on email marketing. The fact that we were sending a physical letter through the post got the attention of our prospects, at a time that their inboxes were overflowing with spam emails.

---

### A moment to reflect

We've covered a wide range of activities yet have barely scratched the surface of each type of marketing. At this stage, the main takeaway should be that there are numerous ways to promote your business, and that there is no 'one size fits all'. Have a think about the types of marketing that you think could work for your business, and as such deserve further consideration and investigation.

# Making a marketing plan

Now that we've considered the different tactics that you can employ to promote a business, it's really important that we look at how some order and management can be put into place. After all, the easiest way to waste a marketing budget is to try different tactics in a scattershot manner, not monitor the results, and ultimately not have any idea of the return on investment.

A marketing plan doesn't need to be overly complicated, and there are no defined formats for how a plan should be structured. I personally prefer marketing plans to be split by month, so that seasonal promotions can be addressed, and to include the details outlined in Table 8.1.

You can see that these details are fairly simple to collate and can be included in a larger plan – perhaps on an Excel spreadsheet with each activity being a new row, and each heading (Activity Name, Theme, etc) being a separate column.

This example was designed to demonstrate the power of tracking through the use of voucher codes. Many businesses will send

**Table 8.1** Example details within a marketing plan

| | |
|---|---|
| **Activity name** | January 'new year' leaflets with a £10 voucher code |
| **Theme/campaign** | New Year, New You campaign |
| **Budgeted spend** | £500 |
| **Budgeted activity** | 10,000 leaflets distributed |
| **Actual spend** | £80 print, £50 design, £350 distribution (total £480) |
| **Actual activity** | 10,000 distributed |
| **Results** | 50 voucher codes redeemed |
| **Return on investment** | £520 (50 vouchers at £20 profit after discount per customer, less £480 cost of promotion) |

leaflets without a clear CTA (call to action), and without any form of accountability – the challenge being that they can never really understand whether the marketing campaign has been successful or not.

Another point to consider is the hidden cost of many marketing activities. You can see in the above example that while the leaflets only cost £80 to print, there was a significant cost in the distribution of the leaflets, and also a design cost to get the leaflets to a point that they could be printed. A common mistake in many marketing plans is forgetting all of the costs and efforts needed to complete a campaign – for example, including the main cost of a stand at an exhibition, but not the cost of transport, promotion teams, electricity, promotional literature and internet access.

A very useful exercise is to double-check the total 'actual spend' on your plan against the total marketing cost in your financial records, to ensure that every spend is being recorded. If not, the return on investment is likely to be inaccurate.

---

### A moment to reflect

A marketing plan is only useful if it ties in with your end goals for the business, and if it is actually used. When you prepare your marketing plan, please make sure that you tie back the expected results from the marketing activities, and the expected cost of the marketing activities, to the budgets and projections that you created as part of your business planning process. Once you know that these stack up – USE IT! A marketing plan that is full of plans but no action isn't worth the paper it's written on.

## Chapter 8 summary

In this chapter we have thought about the concept of a 'customer avatar' and considered some questions that we should ask to understand what the ideal customer looks like. We have considered a variety of marketing tactics and looked at how a marketing plan could be pulled together.

Before proceeding to the next chapter, you should:

1  Think about all of the reflective questions within the chapter.

2  Download and review the Chapter 8 supplementary material from www.carlreader.com/bossit

3  Answer the following questions:

o  When will you commit to thinking about your ideal customer avatar? Revisit the section in the chapter and make a note of the questions that you feel would be appropriate to consider.

_____

_____

_____

_____

o  Which marketing tactics feel like they could be suitable for your business? Set a date to research them more thoroughly, so that you can use them intelligently. Also, make a note of how you intend to track the results of each activity (what are the key performance indicators of each task?).

_____

_____

_____

_____

_____

o  When will you commit to preparing a first draft of a marketing plan for your business?

_____

_____

# 09
# Moving towards the bigger picture
## Scaling your business

In this chapter you will:

- discover a model for scaling a business;
- learn about the basics of customer service and customer fit;
- find out about the basics of recruiting team members;
- find out about the basics of financial management.

In the last chapter we looked at how you can find your customers, by designing a customer avatar and creating a marketing plan. That's great, but to have a successful business you need to consider how you will *keep* your customers, and how you will keep your business alive.

You might also be thinking, 'Is this it?'

Running a new business isn't easy, and while you can take on new customers and build systems, you need to take a wider view on how to manage and lead your business to scale it effectively.

Scaling might seem like a scary word – after all, it is management jargon – but even if your plans are only to take your business from needing you seven days a week to only needing you five days a week, you will need to adopt the role of a business owner to build it in such a way so that you have that freedom. The key principles are the same, whether you are looking to grow to a team of five or a team of 500.

## How do you scale a business?

At its heart, scaling a business is simple. There are four areas that you need to have a plan for, which all interact with each other and the central vision for the business (see Figure 9.1). We will run through them briefly below, but don't worry if the descriptions include phrases that you haven't come across before. All will be explained in Part Four of the book – this is just to set the scene of what we need to consider going forward.

**Figure 9.1** The vision and the four areas to plan for

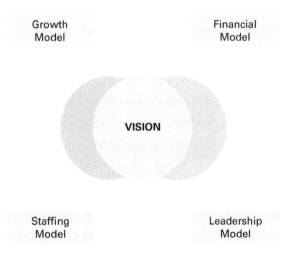

Growth Model

Financial Model

VISION

Staffing Model

Leadership Model

## Vision

This should form the central part of your scaling plan. Without a crystal-clear vision, it will be very difficult to implement any of the plans that you may make in the next four areas – and ultimately, this is why you would embark on any plan to scale the business. The vision should tie in to your personal goals and set the 'big picture' for the other areas to feed into.

## Growth model

This should set out how you want to grow the business. It may be through acquisition, organic growth, franchising, or a number of other ways. It will set out your route to market and the way that you are going to capture market share.

## Financial model

This will set out how the business can finance its growth. The model may include debt financing, private equity, venture capital funding, or even self-funding if the business is generating enough cash.

## Staffing model

This will set out how the business finds and manages the people to grow, to the point of having a management team. It will involve things such as the organization chart, recruitment policies and roles and responsibilities.

## Leadership model

The final part of the jigsaw is the leadership model, which takes the business from an organization run by the founder to a business that runs by itself. It sets out how the team and culture are developed so that everyone is fighting for the same cause, and how the business can ultimately become a separate, saleable asset for its shareholders or owners.

---

### A moment to reflect

The above model is very generic and can be applied to any scaling scenario. It will help you develop the business going forward, but it won't necessarily help you patch up any fundamental issues within a business. If a business is lacking in certain areas, these will need addressing before any formal steps are taken to scale the business. After all, you wouldn't keep filling up a leaky bucket!

---

We will address the scaling model over the next few chapters, but first there are a number of things that need to be considered before moving forward.

## Are the customers the right customers for the business?

Not all revenue is good revenue.

Sometimes, especially in the early days of running a business, we are tempted to accept customers of all shapes and sizes, provided that they have money and a pulse. While this approach can help pay the bills at the very start of a business, it might not necessarily be the best idea to continue to work with all and sundry.

We considered the ideal customer avatar in the last chapter, and the kind of questions that we should ask ourselves about what our ideal customer looks like. Now that we have some customers on board, it is worth sanity-checking this avatar with some common-sense questions, based on actual customer activity:

- Is this customer **loyal**? Are they likely to return and repurchase, or are they a transient customer?
- Is this customer **profitable**? Do we actually make money from serving them?
- Is this customer **pleasant**? Do we enjoy working with them, or do we dread every conversation?
- Is this customer **honest**? Do their values sit in line with our own values?

It might seem idealistic to be able to sack customers in the early days of a business, but we need to be conscious that bad customers only tend to get worse. Also, we need to bear in mind that as a business owner, you benefit directly from working with them if they aren't pleasant but are profitable. Your future staff members might have a very different perspective!

## How do we keep the good customers?

Once we've confirmed that our customers are the kind of customers that we'd like to keep working with, we then need to think about how we keep them coming back again and again. Fundamentally, we can do this in two ways – making sure that they are happy and finding ways to generate loyalty.

In Chapter 7, I explained that I don't tend towards having a 'customer service' system, as I feel that it should come through in every process within the business. You might have decided that you would like to have a separate system for customer service – either way, some of these comments will prove useful regardless of where they are placed within your organization.

Creating a customer service culture within a business, and embedding it within your stakeholders (those who rely on the business), your values and your vision is one of the easiest ways to ensure that customer service is at the centre of what you do and how you do it; and by getting it right from day one, you will be able to ensure that the legacy is continued by your employees as the business grows.

Some of you may have heard about the fabled Nordstrom 'employee manual' which allegedly consisted of one line:

> *Use your best judgment in all situations. There will be no additional rules.*

Unfortunately, this is a myth – the lawyers and personnel teams have had their own way and constructed a 7,000-word manual – but the principles of this one line can serve any business looking to ensure that customer service is at the heart of what they do. By empowering teams that are focused in the same direction, and that are engaged with the organization, you can be sure that they will make the right decision. That stuff might prove to be down the line for many prospective business owners reading this, but you will find that staff will absorb and learn the culture from you. Customer service comes from the top!

The way we do things has also been changed by the wider world. Sometimes, there is a misalignment between what you think the customer will find acceptable and what they actually expect – as their expectations have now been shaped by some of the tech giants. A great example of this misalignment can be found from a viral image that is often shared on social media, quoting something along the lines of:

> We offer three kinds of service
> GOOD – CHEAP – FAST
> But you can only pick two:
> Good and Cheap won't be Fast.
> Fast and Good won't be Cheap.
> Cheap and Fast won't be Good.

While this might have been true in days gone by, we need to keep in mind that we are now rated against the likes of Google and Amazon, rather than against similar businesses to ours. I think

I can safely say on behalf of all end users that Google isn't just good, cheap and fast – it's excellent, free of charge and immediate! On that basis, we need to bear in mind that what worked a decade or two ago might not resonate with the market nowadays, and the beauty of customer service is in the eye of the beholder. Being mindful of how we are rated nowadays – immediacy of response and speed of dispatch being the two most notable factors – means that we can shape our customer service propositions around what today's customer has been led to expect.

The obvious way of checking whether your customer service is hitting the spot is to simply ask them! Customer surveys can take many forms; however, I'm of the belief that there should be minimal friction in the process. In other words, you need to make it as easy as possible to complete, and offer some form of incentive for completion. I personally prefer email or text message surveys (as opposed to in-person or postal surveys), with as few questions as possible. These can simply be 'yes/no' surveys, or you may prefer to use a scoring system such as the net promoter score system.

There are some less obvious ways of keeping track of customer satisfaction, too. Monitoring metrics such as average customer spend (how much do returning customers spend with you?), churn rate (what percentage of customers do you lose?), and customer referral rates (how many new customers come as a recommendation from others?) can help guide you towards general satisfaction levels. Unfortunately, the most useful metrics to use will differ for each business, and without ways of tracking these things, such as loyalty schemes or customer referral discounts, it is difficult to monitor the ratios.

## What happens if it all goes wrong?

For many businesses, a bad customer service experience is inevitable. Despite our best efforts, sometimes we just won't meet the expectations of the customer. It may be that they were over-promised to during the sales process, or possibly that they had an unrealistic idea of what they were buying. It may even be something totally out of everybody's control – such as the weather or external changes. Regardless, when it goes wrong, it is vital that as a business owner you do the right thing for you and the customer.

You might have heard of the saying 'the customer is always right'. While this comes from good intentions, nowadays it is unfortunately used by some as leverage in the social media age. Before the advent of the internet and chat forums, social media platforms and review websites, a bad experience could only have been shared amongst the friends and contacts of a complainant. Now, a one-star review can be seen by thousands.

As a business owner, this will seem unfair, and it is – some people know that they can threaten bad reviews to get a discount and that it could have a tangible impact on your business. Despite this, it is important that you remain pragmatic and realistic when a customer complains.

The first thing that you need to do in these circumstances is honestly appraise the situation and attempt to take the conversation offline, professionally and quickly. If you as the business owner were at fault, try to work with the customer to find a resolution – and update your processes to make sure that it can't happen again. Often, most complainants just want to ensure that no one else experiences the same issues. If it is a false complaint, you have a few options:

- **Leave the review on the website without response** – if a negative review is unfair but not particularly derogatory, you need to decide whether you are able to respond appropriately and professionally, without making yourself appear spiteful. It's a tough balance, and sometimes it is worth leaving the review as is, particularly if the reviewer has portrayed themselves badly.

- **Respond courteously** – sometimes it is worth responding, whether to clarify matters of fact, or to address fake negative reviews. It isn't unheard of for competitors to post fake reviews online, and responding to show that you have no note of their customer record could be appropriate. Regardless of the content of the complaint, there is little point in starting a tit-for-tat battle over the minutiae of their complaint, as it won't do your reputation any favours.

- **Report the complaint** – if the complaint is abusive, libellous, or constitutes a cyber attack, consider reporting the complaint to the website provider.

Regardless of the route that you decide to take, make sure that you lose the red mist and sleep on it first! The keyboard warrior in us all tends to relax after a night's sleep, and being professional is the only course of action that can benefit your business.

# Finding your first staff member

If everything goes well, you should not only be finding new customers, but keeping them too – and pretty soon, you'll need an extra pair of hands!

## *Common mistakes*

We'll cover staffing in far more detail in Chapter 13, but for now I would like to share some of the common mistakes that I see business owners make in recruitment:

### Mistake: Hiring on skills rather than attitude

Without doubt, this is the 'rookie' mistake that all business owners make at some point. They are wowed by an amazing CV, with lots of industry-relevant experience and qualifications. The only problem is... there's a reason why this person has hopped from job to job! As a general rule, skills can be taught but attitude can't be, and the usual cycle for these situations is that an employee is hired on their skills but fired for their attitude after an expensive mistake for both sides. Rather than digging your heels in for a certain minimum skillset, make sure that you are happy with how they will do the job, and why they will go to work for you every day.

### Mistake: Setting arbitrary standards

Despite the legislation designed to stop discrimination, and the common-sense approach of widening your talent pool as far as possible, some employers tend to gravitate towards 'people like them' – whether that is gender, social class, age, or any other factor. This usually isn't a conscious decision, rather simply the result of not proactively attempting to prevent it. Instead, look to widen your search as much as possible. Think about whether you really need to dictate certain educational requirements or experiences. Not only does it keep you on the right side of equality legislation, it also truly benefits your business – allowing you to have diversity of thoughts and ideas, as well as making sure that talented potential staff members don't slip through the net through no fault of their own.

### Mistake: Hiring quickly, firing slowly

The final mistake that I see all the time is when business owners recruit far too quickly. As a general rule, it is not easy to let go of an employee, and depending on where you are there are certain steps that you are legally obliged to follow – not to mention, it's just not a pleasant thing to do. Hiring quickly is often a result of a failure to plan for when the first employee is needed, and when there is too much work but not enough people, businesses can easily be tempted by the first candidate, whether they are suitable or not. Instead, plan for your employment properly and make sure that you really are satisfied with any new recruit before taking them on. By getting it right at the recruitment stage, you will save a lot of headaches down the line.

## Juggling the finances

There is little point in taking on staff if you can't afford to pay them! And perhaps more to the point, your business will not be a success if you cannot manage your cash flow.

I'm sure that you've all heard of the saying:

*Turnover is Vanity, Profit is Sanity, but Cash is King.*

When running a growing business, it can be easy to get blinded by large sales numbers; however, there is so much more that goes into ensuring that a business is successful from a financial perspective.

## *The financial basics*

In Chapter 5, we superficially covered some of the reports that are required for a successful business plan. We'll revisit these now, with an emphasis on how they relate to the financial management of your business. This section will also act as an initial guide before Chapter 12, where we focus on how you can design your funding platform going forward.

Important note: these layouts will differ between regions.

## *Profit and loss account*

This is simply a summary of what you have earned versus what you have spent. It doesn't include all cash transactions – instead, it includes some items that are 'non cash' (such as the depreciation of assets over time), and includes transactions on the date that the transaction happened, not the date that cash was paid.

An example profit and loss account might look like the one in Table 9.1 for a very simple business.

Now, the example in Table 9.1 is only a very basic statement, but it will give you an idea of how a profit and loss account should look. I haven't included regional-specific items, nor have I included many accounting adjustments – it is simply a basic example of how a business can report its profit over a period of time.

The profit and loss account will give you a number of key statistics that you should keep an eye on. In this example, the gross profit and the net profit are two key numbers. Rather than just

**Table 9.1** Profit and loss statement

| | £/$/€ | £/$/€ |
|---|---|---|
| **Turnover**<br>*The total of sales made, exclusive of sales tax/VAT* | | 100,000 |
| **Less: Cost of sales**<br>*Costs directly allocated to sales, such as product purchases. This calculation will also take into account the movement of stock and/or the value of work in progress in the period, by including stock held at the start of the period and deducting stock held at the end.* | | |
| Opening stock | 2,000 | |
| Purchases of products during the year | 30,000 | |
| Less: closing stock | −7,000 | |
| | | −25,000 |
| **Gross Profit**<br>*Turnover less the cost of sales* | | 75,000 |
| **Less: Overheads**<br>*Costs not directly related to sales. Could include items such as rent, business rates, marketing, administration staff, etc.* | | |
| Rent | 6,000 | |
| Business rates | 3,000 | |
| Staff wages | 20,000 | |
| Marketing costs | 5,000 | |
| Repairs and renewals | 500 | |
| Sundry expenses | 500 | |
| | | −35,000 |
| **Net profit** | | 40,000 |

tracking the total value of these, business owners would tend to track the percentages (otherwise known as margins):

**Gross profit margin:**
$$\frac{\text{Gross profit x } 100 = (\%)}{\text{Turnover}}$$

**Net profit margin:**
$$\frac{\text{Net profit x } 100 = (\%)}{\text{Turnover}}$$

In this example, the gross profit margin would be 75% and the net profit margin would be 40%. Understanding these percentages is far more important as the business grows, as you will be able to check that the business is continuing to operate at the same level of profitability.

---

### A moment to reflect

While the absolute numbers are important, it is also vital to track the right ratios in your business. If we were to fast-forward this business to year 2, and imagine that the business is making £500,000 of sales but only £100,000 of gross profit, that would be a major warning sign. Sure, the monetary value of gross profit is £25,000 higher, but the reality is that the business has gone from making 75% margin on each sale down to 20%. This would be a sign of extreme discounting, a change of market to a far less profitable market, or very poor management. Either way, it will make the business much more fragile and susceptible to external issues and changes.

---

The two margins are not the only thing that a business should track. Each business will have its own metrics that it needs to monitor – in this example, stock would probably be an area of concern – and the balance that the business owner needs to find is that of monitoring the key numbers but not being consumed by the detail.

## The balance sheet

The balance sheet is effectively a 'snapshot' of a business's asset value at any one time: it summarizes what is *owned* versus what is *owed*. It will include all 'fixed assets', which are items that are owned for more than a year, and 'current assets', which covers assets that are fast moving, such as cash at the bank and the value of your stock and debtors. After deducting liabilities, it will show the net worth of the business.

Table 9.2 shows a basic example balance sheet.

You will see here that the **net assets** balances with the **financed by** section, showing effectively what the business is worth on paper before the value of the trade is introduced.

Some of the key things that business owners should be looking out for here are:

- **Liquidity:** are there sufficient 'liquid assets' – such as cash – to pay any immediate debts?

- **Dead assets:** are we including assets such as stock which are outdated, and hence worthless?

- **Missing liabilities:** are there any business debts that, for whatever reason, aren't showing up on the financial reports?

- **Cash balance:** is there enough cash, or available working capital/overdraft, to continue to trade uninterrupted?

---

### A moment to reflect

Perhaps you haven't started in business to become an accountant, but it will really help you grow a business if you can get to grips with these basics. If you've just skim-read the above examples, I would urge you to work through the models more carefully, to ensure that you are comfortable with the terminology used. It is likely that your bankers, accountant and any investors will expect you to be able to understand these phrases, these reports, and how they apply to your business.

**Table 9.2** Balance sheet

| | £/$/€ | £/$/€ |
|---|---|---|
| **Fixed assets**<br>*The value of assets that are kept by the business for a long time. This will include things such as computers, machinery, property and motor vehicles. Usually, these assets have 'depreciation' or 'amortization' against them to reflect the spreading of their cost over time.* | | |
| Motor vehicles | 20,000 | |
| Fixtures and fittings | 10,000 | |
| | | **30,000** |
| **Current assets**<br>*Turnover less the cost of sales* | | |
| **Less: Overheads**<br>*Owned but not long-term assets, such as cash at the bank and the value of debtors. It may also include the value of any stock held, or work in progress completed at the time of preparation.* | | |
| Cash at bank | 10,000 | |
| Stock | 7,000 | |
| | | **17,000** |
| **Total assets** | | **47,000** |
| **Current liabilities**<br>*Includes any debt repayable either immediately, or within one year. You will also see the short-term element of any longer-term debt, eg bank loans, in this section.* | | |
| Trade creditors | 5,000 | |
| Directors loan account | 1,000 | |
| | | **−6,000** |
| **Total assets less current liabilities** | | **41,000** |

*(continued)*

**Table 9.2** (Continued)

|  | £/$/€ | £/$/€ |
|---|---|---|
| **Long-term liabilities** <br> *In this example, there are no long-term liabilities, but this is where you would expect to see things such as bank loans, hire purchase agreements, and other forms of structured debt.* |  | **0** |
| **Net assets** <br> *Total assets, less total liabilities. In other words, the 'asset' value of the business. Typically less than a purchaser would pay for a business, as it doesn't account for the value of the trading.* |  | **41,000** |
| **Financed by** <br> *How the business has financed its net asset position* |  |  |
| Profit and loss account | 40,000 |  |
| Share capital | 1,000 |  |
|  |  | **41,000** |

# Other reports

The profit and loss account and the balance sheet are often quoted as the two important financial reports, and are often the main reports required by law. However, there are other reports that can help you run your business at a practical level.

## Cash flow forecasts

While these might seem complex, they can be as simple as a note of how much cash you have in the bank and what bills you have to pay. That's clearly a very simple cash flow forecast, but amazingly, I see some businesses who don't even know that basic information! Businesses don't tend to die because of the details in their financial reports… it ultimately comes down to a lack of cash to service their debts and costs. By having a report that can keep you on top of your cash position, you will be well placed to avoid any bumps in the road.

## Period comparison reports

The standard reports as described above are useful as part of a wider picture, but often can be confusing in isolation. By monitoring monthly income and expenditure, against the same month of the previous year, you will be able to identify any trends and become aware of whether the performance is what you should be expecting.

## Budget versus actual reports

Again, this report will help supplement the information that is included within the retrospective reports. By comparing the business performance against what you had planned, you can see if you are on track to reach your projected goals and adjust if necessary.

---

### A moment to reflect

Have a think about the way that you would prefer to digest this information. Not all of us are predisposed to reading page after page of numbers. Would graphs, or perhaps a 'traffic light' system of red, yellow and green, help focus your attention on the important statistics? Have a chat with your financial expert to see how your management reports can be tailored so that they work for you.

---

## Chapter 9 summary

In this chapter we have taken a whistle-stop tour across the basics of scaling a business, by looking at the foundations that you will need in place. We've looked at hiring team members, and the financial jargon that you will need to understand. We've also touched on customer service and my scaling model.

Before proceeding to the next chapter, you should:

1 Think about all of the action points within the chapter.

2 Download and review the Chapter 9 supplementary material from www.carlreader.com/bossit

3 Answer the following question:

o What areas of this chapter seemed daunting to you? The stuff that we've talked about here might seem like it is a little way off, but it can come back to haunt you very quickly. We have also covered a lot of ground, with each of the topics being worthy of a book themselves. Make a note of any topics that you would like to dig a little deeper into, so that you can start to create a learning action list.

_____

_____

_____

# Part Four
# Scale it

# 10

# An introduction to scaling

In this chapter you will:

- understand the importance of a compelling vision;
- learn how the vision should be articulated and communicated;
- learn about how the vision can be woven into every part of your business;
- understand the importance of continual review and improvement.

**W**ell done! If you've followed the steps in the book so far, you will have the groundwork for a successful business – one which hopefully allows you to ditch the day job and focus on the business full-time. You might even be able to get to the point of employing a couple of team members, or considering other business opportunities.

That's a great place to be in, and is where the vast majority of successful businesses get to. With the rise in the gig economy and the freelance world, most businesses are made up of the proprietor and possibly an assistant.

But this may not be your end goal.

Many people want their business to work for them, rather than working for their business. Instead of having what is effectively a job with uncertain income and unsociable hours, they want a business that can give them the luxury of going away on holiday, taking time out and growing without them.

This is only possible if you turn your self-employment into a scalable business.

# What makes a business scalable?

In the last chapter we looked at the fundamental parts that a business needs to have in place to be scalable – the vision, the growth model, the financial model, the staffing model and the leadership model (see Figure 10.1).

We will cover all of these in this part of the book, but I'd also like to touch on the characteristics of a scalable business: the stuff that the outside world sees, beyond the conscious models that a business owner would put into place.

## *A lack of dependency on the owner*

This is perhaps the biggest indication of a business that has become scalable. Rather than the owner of the business doing all of the jobs, from cleaning in the morning to closing up at night, the business

**Figure 10.1** The vision and the four areas to plan for

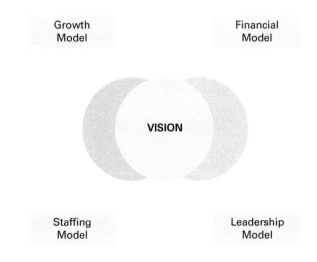

Growth
Model

Financial
Model

**VISION**

Staffing
Model

Leadership
Model

works by itself. Staff are free to run the business in the way it should be run, and have authority to make decisions as if it was their business, in accordance with any set guidelines.

## The absence of bottlenecks

Another key feature of a scalable business is that there are no bottlenecks in the business. Smaller businesses tend to rely initially on the owner, and then on key staff members. As these team members get overloaded, the work stacks up. Calls go unanswered and customers are let down. A scalable business has usually identified these bottlenecks and proactively looks to reduce their occurrence in the business.

## Systems that just 'work'

Rather than staff having to work out what to do in each situation that they encounter, the business has already planned for the next couple of milestones ahead. The internal processes and procedures are as watertight as can be, and are also able to handle a dramatic increase in the business's activity.

## Acting bigger than today

Scalable businesses tend to act as if they are where they want to be. Rather than using the free-of-charge version of critical software, they invest in the right solution. Job descriptions, roles and responsibilities and other documents are in place and used, rather than reliance on knowing the individuals in the business. The business is run 'properly'.

## A culture of growth

Instead of being happy with their lot, staff members are enthused by the opportunity that the business has. They know that they are part of a journey that is bigger than them and they are grateful for the opportunity to be on the bus. The growth of the business coincides with their personal growth and everybody in the team is aligned and pointing in the same direction.

For a business that is just starting out, a lot of this might seem to be a bit of a pipe dream. After all, there are far more important balls to juggle at that stage: getting customers, serving customers and paying the bills are often the sole focus of a business at the early stages. Once the business is stable, though, the choice of where to go next comes up.

## Should you scale your business?

Before any business owner dives into the nuts and bolts of scaling their business, it is wise to step back and think about the vision for scaling the business.

You might remember very early on in the book that we talked about the four key steps for any business to go through:

DREAM    PLAN    DO    REVIEW

When it comes to running a business, these steps should be followed as a cycle – it isn't enough to do it once and forget about it. Businesses grow and develop over time, and so should the dream, the plan, the actions and the management of the process.

Preparing the vision for scaling is effectively revisiting the dream. But hopefully this time with some miles on the clock and experience along the way!

One of the things that always makes me smile when speaking to new business owners is just how bright-eyed and bushy-tailed people can be about their new business idea. Sales projections are usually much higher than they should be, the marketplace will of course welcome their idea with open arms, and the wind will always be behind them.

At the point of scaling a business, an entrepreneur will have been through more than a fair share of battles along the way. It's likely that they'll have suffered bad debts, been let down by suppliers, and had times when there is simply 'more month than money'.

While these experiences are painful at the time, they do help shape the considerations that are needed to decide whether scaling a business is right for both the business and the entrepreneur.

## A moment to reflect

Have a think about other areas in your life that have been shaped by previous experiences. It might be evident in the way that you approach romantic relationships, buying decisions, or health matters. It is likely that some negative experiences in your life have helped you become more aware of what you want and, more importantly, what you don't want. When setting a vision for scaling a business, it is critical that you go into it with your eyes open – in particular, with the full awareness of what you don't want from the new and enlarged business. Does more of the same seem appealing to you?

If you've spent some time thinking about this, you'll probably realize that there are a number of personal risks when it comes to scaling a business. It's not simply a case of finding more customers and selling more stuff – you need to transform your business so that it has the characteristics that we described earlier in this chapter, and the foundations of the scaling model covered in this part. It will most likely take a toll on your personal life, your work–life balance, and possibly on your health and relationships.

Not only that, you will find that your work life will change dramatically. Rather than doing the doing, you will go through the process of becoming a manager, and on to a leader. It might be that you set up your business – let's use an example of a car mechanic business – because you loved tinkering with cars. As the business scales, your role will move through that of managing a team of mechanics, administrators, and service representatives, and into a board-level executive leading a management team towards the bigger picture.

Finally, you need to remember that you may well not be the boss, and depending on the type of funding raised, you might not even stay on the journey of scaling! A research piece for *Harvard Business Review*,[1] The Founder's Dilemma, studied 212 American startups in the dot-com boom and found that 50 per cent of founders were no longer the CEO after three years, and fewer than 25 per cent led their company's IPOs (initial public offerings). These exits weren't voluntary, and for every Mark Zuckerberg (Facebook) and Sara Blakely (Spanx) who successfully lead their businesses from idea to global domination, there are countless casualties who didn't survive the journey.

# Setting the vision for the business

Regardless of whether you are planning global domination, or simply growing your business beyond where it is today, it is important that you have a clear vision of where you want your business to go. The challenge that most entrepreneurs encounter is that their ambitions are matched by a very fuzzy vision of what success means to them – without being able to clearly articulate the vision to others, it is unlikely that you will get the funding from external sources or the buy-in from the team needed to start the journey of scaling.

I find that a really useful way of helping to clarify a vision is to ask some probing exploratory questions to understand what the business owner is trying to achieve:

**What difference do you want to make in the world?** Do you simply want to sell more stuff, or make a deeper change? Will the business fight a bigger mission – alleviating poverty, caring for the environment, or representing certain causes? Will the business be known as a leading example of staff engagement and satisfaction? What mark will the business make in the world?

**What size would you like the business to be?** Are your aims regional, national, or international? Do you have a goal in mind, whether revenue, staff numbers, or number of units sold? Is there a comparative business that you'd like to be held in the same esteem as?

**What is the end goal for you as the founder?** Do you have 'the number' in mind that you would walk away from the business for? Are you looking to build a legacy or a pension? Are you scaling the business to fulfil your own personal need, or the business's potential?

**What do you want from the business as it grows?** Are you looking to take more cash out of the business as it grows, or build the cheque on exit? Are you looking to work harder in the business, or take a step back?

**Where do you see yourself in the organization?** Do you need to be 'top of the tree'? Could you accept a new CEO being appointed, while you work as part of the team? Would you be happy to sidestep into an 'evangelical' role, being a face for the business, while others run it for you?

---

## A moment to reflect

Try to spend some time exploring these questions. Some of them are relatively easy to answer, but others are designed to dive deeper into your psyche to help you understand what drives you as a business owner, a team member and an entrepreneur. There are no right or wrong answers, provided that the answers you give are truthful! Your vision has to be congruent with what you want to achieve in the business and in the world. There is little point setting a vision to end human trafficking, for example, if your sole motivation is cash in the bank. Don't answer in the way that you feel society would like you to answer – make sure that your answers fit with who you are and what you want. That is the *only* way to ensure that you have the right answer to a question!

Once you have answered these reflective questions, you should be a little closer towards understanding where you want yourself and the business to go. Some of your answers may have been quite woolly, whereas I'm sure that others will have been very specific. It's now time to start clarifying the vision a little more, so that you have some facts and figures to go alongside the feelings. Use some of the answers that you have from the above exercise to help supplement your answers here – for example, if you have an idea of your target revenue, you should be able to calculate roughly the staffing numbers and profitability, based on your understanding of how a business in the industry should work:

- What revenue will the business generate each year?
- Which locations will the business operate in?
- What will be the business's largest geographical market?
- What industries will the business serve?
- What will be the main product or service of the business?
- Who will the business's ideal customer be?
- How many staff will the business have?
- Why will the staff come to work for the business?
- What will the values of the business be?
- What is the one thing that the business will do better than its competitors?
- What will the business be known for?
- Why will the customers buy from you?
- What will the profitability of the business be?
- Will the business be owned by you or will it be split between third parties and/or investors?
- If you are a partnership, will that partnership continue through the scaling process?
- Will your current employees be the team of the future? If not, why not?

- What is the exit plan for the business? Trade sale? Stock market flotation? Other?

- How long will the business run until your exit plan is executed?

- If the business was to be compared to a global business outside of your industry, who would it be and why?

- If the business was to be compared to a supermarket, which one would you choose and why?

- If the business was to be compared to a car, which one would it be and why?

These clarifying questions will help you drill down into a clearer picture of what the end picture looks like for the business.

---

### A moment to reflect

By this stage, I would hope that you have a clearer idea of the end goal for the business. Please remember that no dream is final, and that they need to keep evolving – however, the general direction can't change too many times without unsettling staff, customers and investors. If you have only skimmed through the questions, perhaps because you don't feel ready to answer them, I encourage you to revisit them and answer as best you can. Scaling might not be right for you just now, but the questions will help provoke a different way of thinking about your business, which might empower you to think about how to do things differently and ultimately lay the pathway towards scaling.

---

## I have a plan – what now?

Once you have gone through the vision-setting exercises, you should have some idea of the detail behind where you want the business to go. That's great, but simply designing a dream isn't going to help you move towards it. You will remember much of this from the dreaming and planning process when starting the business and there's no point in reinventing the wheel here: if you'd like to revisit how to create an effective plan, and how to produce business plans, you can revisit the earlier chapters in the book, as the advice doesn't change.

There is, however, one big difference now. You have a business.

You have customers, and possibly a team. There are people who rely on your business doing what it does, in the way that it does it today. You might have a business loan to repay and you may well be living on some of the profits of the business.

Setting out a dream and a plan is relatively risk-free in the early days, but you need to be very careful once you already have a business to ensure that you don't disrupt the magic that you have already created.

Cast your mind back to being an employee. You probably remember times that were particularly unsettling. New announcements about how the business is changing. New managers being appointed. These kinds of things can really unsettle a team, not to mention customers.

As you can imagine, announcing a dream without a plan of communication, let alone a plan of implementation, can be unsettling and indeed detrimental to the business. On that basis, we need to consider who the stakeholders of the business are, so that a strategy for sharing the vision can be formed.

## Managing your stakeholders

Simply put, a stakeholder can be anyone who encounters some level of impact from the business. The obvious stakeholders for most businesses would be the staff and the shareholders; however, for most businesses the stakeholders extend beyond those involved within the business. Stakeholders can include the customers and suppliers of a business, the industry that the business operates in, the markets which the business serves, and the community that the business resides in.

**CASE STUDY**   d&t stakeholders

For my core business, d&t, we underwent an exercise of brainstorming our stakeholders.

At first, we decided that we didn't want to use the term 'stakeholders', as it seemed to be far too corporate compared with how we normally do things. Despite the semantics, we continued to explore who we serve as a business, and put together the 'Five Stars' of d&t (Figure 10.2).

**Figure 10.2**   d&t stars (stakeholders)

STAFF

CLIENTS                                MARKETS

INDUSTRY              COMMUNITY

As you can see, we decided to put our staff at the top of the star, on the basis that if we get our staff engagement right, the service to all other stakeholders would inevitably follow. Next up, we have our customers and markets. We clearly have to look after the customers who pay for our services; however, we believed that we also had an obligation to serve the markets in which we operated. We did this by attending industry events, and I engaged in thought leadership and served on the trade association as a director and committee member. Finally, we had our community and industry – which we served through helping fundraise for charity and by leading the conversation in the accounting world, giving back to the industry that allowed us to build a great business by helping others learn from what went well and what didn't for us.

---

**A moment to reflect**

This is a great time to have a think about the stakeholders in your business, both currently (to help you understand who your vision needs to be communicated to) and in the future. You don't need to adopt the 'five stars' format, but what I would ask is that you make a list of every single group impacted by your business and highlight the key groups within that.

---

By having your stakeholders clearly defined, you will be able to work out how best to communicate your vision with them.

Putting the exercise about stakeholders to one side, it's important to know that the vision really does permeate throughout the business. The obvious impact is on the company's culture, which we will cover in more detail within Chapters 13 and 14 when we discuss staffing and leadership; however, in my opinion, the vision is the foundation that underpins all of the factors of scaling a business. It determines your growth model, it is the key to success for funding, and naturally has a massive impact on your culture and values as a business.

Now that you know the importance of a vision in your business when looking to scale, you must also remember the importance of communicating it correctly. Before shouting about your grand plans to your team members, I would highly recommend working through the next four chapters to make sure that you have clarity on the right way to scale. This will allow you to confidently answer any tricky questions that might arise from team members as well as allow you to sanity-check your plans.

## What if this doesn't feel right?

We need to face the reality that not all businesses are suitable for scaling, and not all business owners want to scale their business. In this chapter we have stepped up the pace a little and moved from the operational side of running a business into some more strategic aspects. It might be that by doing the exercises, something doesn't sit quite right with you.

If that's the case for you, let me be the first to say – well done.

In business, there is a lot to be said for intuition, and it is vital that you pick up on these signs sooner rather than later. If you are finding it hard to picture your current business scaling up, or you are struggling to really believe the answers that you've come up with for the probing questions, it's a sign that you really should consider this more deeply before pressing ahead.

It might also be a nervous flutter at the thought of external investors taking over the business, or regarding how you can step away and let a management team run the day-to-day operations, doing things that you don't know about for customers you've never met.

Not everyone wants to or is able to grow a business aggressively – and we all have our limits. We touched on the different types of personality early on in the book and looked at the technician versus the manager versus the entrepreneur. There could well be far more divisions between these categories made, as each of us are different. Those of us who are better at starting a business would probably struggle running a unicorn business with a valuation of $1 billion, and conversely, the average board-level executive would struggle to start a business. In between those two levels, there are many 'sweet spots' – for example, I know that I operate best when I have a strong team around me, but also a good level of control. That is the point where my energy has the most impact and I can play to my own strengths.

Before embarking on the scaling journey, make sure that you are prepared for it.

## Chapter 10 summary

In this chapter we have looked in detail at the importance of building a compelling vision before scaling a business. We have considered how the vision will influence each and every part of the business and discussed the need to communicate the vision effectively.

Before proceeding to the next chapter, you should:

1 Think about all of the reflective questions within the chapter.

2 Download and review the Chapter 10 supplementary material from www.carlreader.com/bossit

3 Answer the following questions:

   o Which of the exploratory and probing questions do you need to think about more deeply? Are there any more questions that you feel that you should be asking of yourself and your business? Note them down, and commit to a time to think about these more thoroughly.

   _____
   _____
   _____
   _____

   o Who are the stakeholders in your business? Try to prioritize them, to help you understand the emphasis that should be placed in your communication strategy. Identify any conflicts between stakeholders, and also any stakeholders that might arise in the future once you scale your business.

   _____
   _____
   _____
   _____

   o We touched on the fact that scaling a business isn't right for everyone and for every business. Do you have any concerns or fears at the moment? If so, note them down. While writing them down won't automatically eradicate them, it will provide you with the opportunity to do some more digging in those areas. It might simply be that more knowledge about certain subjects could reduce uncertainty. Alternatively, it might be that you need to bounce around some ideas with your business advisers.

_____

_____

_____

_____

# 11
# Scaling 101 – The growth model

In this chapter you will:

- learn about the different methods of scaling a business;
- understand the pros and cons of different scaling methods;
- think about what could work for your business;
- learn about other factors that might lead to growth.

Now we understand the importance of having a strong vision before scaling a business, we can explore some of the methods that you can use to grow.

In this chapter, we will explore a few of the more common routes to market, and will discuss the advantages and disadvantages of each. There is no magic pill for this – different businesses will benefit from different growth models, and sometimes it comes down to how the entrepreneur operates best. At this stage, all I can suggest is that you gain as much of an understanding as possible about the different options available to you, so that you can make an informed choice about how to grow your business.

# Organic growth

Most businesses start by growing organically and recruiting new customers one by one. This is the natural way that businesses grow, particularly in the early days. Growth is on a customer-by-customer basis, and as more income is received, this is used to fund the marketing for more customers.

That is organic growth at its simplest; however, it doesn't have to be entirely self-funded. Once you have a track record of attracting interest and customers, it is possible to raise funding to grow the business more aggressively. This can either be through bank lending or by finding investors who are willing to put 'rocket fuel' into your business to take it to the next level, and we will discuss some of these options in the next chapter.

It is also one of the least complicated routes to market, as it tends not to involve legal agreements – organic growth is just a case of doing what you do, but faster and faster. This, however, also brings some challenges to the table:

**The time it takes:** often, organic growth is slower than other methods of growing a business. This is because a business needs to invest in its marketing, and will only have a finite resource of cash available to do so. Not only that, the business will need to ensure that it has the capacity to produce the products or provide the service, so it will be juggling the cost of finding new customers alongside the cost of being able to serve them. This is a tricky balancing act for the best of businesses and can lead to the growth being much slower than expected.

**The financial cost:** organic growth depends on investment in marketing and capacity. While a business can self-fund this, the reality is that a business looking to scale up may well need to take on external investment. This investment will come at a cost, with either interest being charged on any debt or equity being given away. The cash cycle for organic growth also means that the outgoings are spent before the customer provides any value to the business, leading to a continual challenge of the pace of growth versus the funds to invest.

**The pressure on operations:** as the business growth is all 'company owned', rather than franchised or licensed, the business will need to employ the team to manage the growth, and in turn the business will need to invest in the management and administration infrastructure to look after the team members.

**Geographical and operational restrictions:** unlike acquisitions, the business needs to capture new market share, which can prove costly. The business may also find that there is a limited 'total addressable market' (TAM), which will mean that the cost of acquisition (CAC) will increase as these new customers become more and more sought after. These limits may be imposed by the geographical area that the business serves or the product mix that it offers.

# Strategic alliances and partnerships

One way to increase the opportunities available to a business is to invest in strategic alliances and partnerships. This is something that I have done personally in my business, and on the face of it, it should be very simple. A successful alliance should be a 'win-win' arrangement, where both sides benefit from working together. I find that service businesses tend to benefit most from these, although complementary product businesses can also benefit. The reality, however, is that while these partnerships can be easy to enter into, they can be very difficult to make successful.

Perhaps the biggest challenge is a lack of motivation to really drive the alliance forward. If the balance of benefits isn't equal, you will find that one side soon loses interest in pushing it forward. While financial remuneration sometimes works, it isn't always the answer. Some referrers prefer not to receive financial compensation and instead look for ways to mutually promote each other's businesses.

There are no real disadvantages with entering into strategic alliances, provided that they are done sensibly. Here are my top tips about entering into these:

**Make sure that you understand the balance of power:** in every partnership, there is an unequal balance of power between the two parties. Even if both businesses are of equivalent size and stature, it is likely that there are some differences between them. Take time to explore the background of both businesses and, perhaps most importantly, the presence that your potential partner has within your marketplace. Often we can be blinded by the appeal of global businesses; however, if they do not have any substantial dealings with the kind of customers that we would like to work with, the partnership may become imbalanced but not in the way that might be expected.

**Remember where you and your partners sit in the food chain:** if you feel that both sides of the partnership have an equal balance of power, you then need to consider where each business sits in the food chain. Sometimes, you simply will not be able to provide as many leads as a partner, just because your service is used after theirs or vice versa. A good example of this would be a website designer and an SEO (search engine optimization) specialist working together. On the face of it, it would seem like a fairly natural partnership; however a business would not need search engine optimization until the website has been designed – and at the point a business approaches someone to promote their new website, they are unlikely to need their website redesigned.

**Test the customer experience:** nothing can strain a strategic alliance more than a mutual customer being let down by a partner. Make sure that you are comfortable that your partner will deal with your customers in the way that you would expect them to be dealt with. When you refer a customer to a third party, your reputation is as much on the line as the partner's – your customers will have built a level of trust in you and your business, and will rely on your opinion that the recommendation is worth taking. If your customer is then let down in any way, it reduces that level of trust.

**Set clear performance expectations of each other:** if you've managed to align yourself insofar as what each of you can offer to the relationship, and are happy about how the partner will look after your customers, the next thing that you need to do is to set some targets for the relationship. This can be really simple – something along the lines of 'let's try to make three decent introductions per month' – or it can be a more formal system of monitoring. Regardless of how you do it, the key thing here is to make sure that both sides are fully aware of what is expected of them.

**Agree boundaries of the relationship:** there is so much more to a partnership than just counting the wins. Just like in a romantic relationship, you need to decide what your boundaries are – and what constitutes cheating! If one of you expects exclusivity in the relationship, while the other expects to share the love, it is likely to cause a lot of tension. Have a chat with your potential partner about how the relationship will work to avoid misunderstandings at the start. Often, if you are the 'lesser' partner in an alliance, it is likely that the referrer will work with other businesses like yours. That's fine, provided that you aren't expecting them to solely refer you. It is also a great opportunity to discuss how you could become the partner of choice, as they may well have only spread referrals previously because the relationships weren't working as they saw that they should.

**Make it easy to refer business to each other:** it might sound obvious, but my last tip is to make it as easy as possible for your partners to refer business to you. If the process is at all sticky for them, their staff, or their customers, it is unlikely that they will be proactive in pushing work your way. By making it as painless as possible, you can ensure that the partnership has the highest chance of success.

# Franchising

Business format franchising is a method of business expansion that allows you to work with franchisees, who set up their own business in a geographical region using your brand, your systems and your culture. Franchising has many different forms, and many global high street brands such as McDonald's, Starbucks and Subway have used it as a growth model, alongside countless smaller businesses in most sectors.

A franchise usually consists of four key assets:

The legal agreement: as the franchisor, the franchise agreement determines the value of your business, so it is not something that you should look to save a few pennies on. It sets out the relationship between you as the franchisor and the franchisee, covering matters such as the term of the agreement, what is expected of the franchisee, how much they pay you (known as the management service fee), and how the relationship can be ended. It's important to take specialist advice on the preparation of the agreement, together with what you need to do as a franchisor, as each country has different levels of regulation over franchises – in the US, for example, franchises are regulated at both a federal and a state level; whereas in the UK, there is no specific franchise legislation and anybody can call themselves a 'franchise'.

The brand: while established brands such as Burger King and Anytime Fitness need no introduction, it is likely that your brand will not be quite at their level of brand recognition. Even so, as a franchisor you need to ensure that the value of your brand is maximized and the use of your brand is controlled. A franchisee would normally expect you to have at least trademarked your brand in their country of operation, so that no one other than franchisees can use it. For your part, you would also expect that the franchisee only uses the brand in the way that you would like, and as such, most franchisors produce brand guidelines setting out exactly what can and can't be done by the franchisee.

The systems: franchising is sometimes referred to as a 'business in a box', and franchisees usually choose to invest in a franchise system instead of starting their own business because they see it as saving them from reinventing the wheel. To help them hit the ground running, you would be expected to provide an operations manual to explain how the business should be run. In the past, operations manuals would have been weighty documents, but nowadays they can take the form of an intranet or a wiki-style document. Regardless, it is still useful to bear in mind the old saying that an operations manual should be a 'loose-leaf binder' rather than a bound hardback book – meaning that the document should be alive and iterative instead of set in stone. Businesses grow over time, and while your operations might be market-leading at the moment, it is important to build the culture of improvement – and the operations manual is where this happens.

The culture: finally, the area that many franchises don't address is the culture – 'the way we do things'. Franchisees are generally looking to buy into something that is bigger and better than what they can create for the same investment, and for me the culture sits alongside the brand and the systems. By running regional and national conferences, franchise advisory councils, and awards events, you can help the franchisees be in business for themselves but not by themselves.

Although the transference of these assets should occur in every franchise operation, there are many things that might differ from franchise to franchise. Usually, networks charge a management service fee based on revenue; however, it is sometimes the case (particularly in cash businesses) that the fee is a fixed amount. The term of the franchise agreement is usually five years, but again this might differ – banks tend to want their loans to expire by the end of the initial franchise term.

One of the usual fears that business owners have about franchising their business is a loss of control. If the business is franchised properly, with appropriate operations manuals and operational control from head office through the use of franchise managers, this shouldn't prove to be too much of an issue. What is potentially an issue is the difference in personality type between employees that the business has employed before and franchisees. Often, franchisees sit somewhere between employees and entrepreneurs, and need some handholding to get to the point where they are able to run the business successfully by themselves.

The other area where businesses tend to get franchising wrong is by neglecting the investment required to franchise properly. It is possible to use 'copy and paste' template systems and agreements, but in my experience, this is often a false economy, as the business foundations need to be robust. After all, the eventual sale value of a franchise network is entirely based on the strength of the brand, systems, and agreements in place! Not only does the infrastructure require investment, but also the recruitment. Each franchisee costs several thousand pounds to find, recruit and set up – and many businesses underestimate the impact that this can have on their cash flow.

If you are considering franchising as a route to expand your business domestically or internationally, my first suggestion would be to get in contact with your national franchise association. The trade bodies tend to have a wealth of information available about the market and will signpost you towards the right advisers to help you on your journey. They will also offer you the opportunity to meet other franchisors who have taken the path before.

There are other similar models, such as licensing and distributorships, which reduce the level of control that the head office has over its partners. A good example of a licensing agreement would be Coca-Cola, who license the use of their brand and recipes internationally, but don't control the operational side of the regional businesses.

## Mergers and acquisitions

A very common growth option for many businesses that are looking to expand quickly is to acquire similar businesses that are operating in their space. While this method clearly requires intensive funding, it allows businesses to capture both market share and staff. Not only that, the group of businesses that results from an acquisition initiative can benefit from sharing a head office infrastructure and from the shared experience across the group.

A business that has pushed ahead with an acquisition strategy also has another benefit to its owners, in that the valuation can increase disproportionately. Naturally the combined profits of the business will be the basis of any valuation, but the price/earnings ratio (see Chapter 12) used will also increase as the business gets bigger, meaning that there are benefits from both sides of the valuation equation.

While this might sound very attractive, there are a few problems that you need to consider too. The first is that when you acquire a business, you don't just acquire the good stuff! You will inherit the culture, the team and the way of doing things, which might not be the same as you would do. You might also find that certain product lines are unprofitable and that customers have a certain perception of the business.

Then there's the possibility that you open yourself up to skeletons in the closet with an acquisition. There are two types of purchase – a share purchase, where you purchase the shares of the company and take on the entire history of the business, and a trade and asset purchase, where you just purchase the 'good stuff' from the business. Regardless of which route you choose, you can put legal warranties in place to protect you from any historic liabilities; however, the practical reality is that if there is anything that can damage the goodwill of the business, you will suffer the reputational impact regardless of the nuances of what the legal agreements contain.

Another thing to bear in mind is that acquisitions can be perceived to be anti-competitive. You are unlikely to unknowingly breach any anti-competition legislation, as the size of any such deal would naturally lead you towards having a strong team behind you who would highlight this risk, but you may find that market sentiment plays against the new enlarged business.

Bearing the above benefits and problems in mind, if you are considering an acquisition strategy, I would advise that you partner with an agent who can help source opportunities for you in your desired target market. They might charge both a retainer and a success fee, but you will find that they will open opportunities and act as a facilitator during the negotiations. In my experience, business acquisitions always have curveballs thrown at some point, and having someone on your team who has been there and seen it several times before will help you separate the negotiation tactics from the real deal breakers.

# Some of the tactics used for growth

The above whistle-stop tour of the different types of growth strategy should give you an idea of some of the options available to you and should help you shape your thoughts around the general direction that you would like to take your growth model in.

I'd now like to touch on a few different tactics that businesses use to increase their revenue.

## *Increasing product/service range*

Regardless of which industry you are in, there is a limit on the number of potential buyers for what you do. The total number is known as the 'total addressable market', and realistically you will only ever be able to convert a percentage of this market into becoming customers. The value of your total addressable market is calculated as the number of potential customers, multiplied by the average customer value. So, perhaps the simplest tactic for growth is to increase the number of potential customers, increase the average customer value, or do both.

One of the ways of doing this is by increasing the range of products or services that you provide to the market. Whereas we've looked at 'horizontal' growth so far, which is doing more of the same, you can also consider 'vertical' growth. This might be a product or service that your current customers are also likely to need. So, for example, a car sales business might decide to start offering car servicing and repairs as well. This tactic can be used in both organic and acquisitive models of growth and helps increase the average value of customers.

## Innovations

Another tactic that some businesses use for growth is innovation. While we tend to think of Silicon Valley and similar environments for innovative companies, innovation is actually all around us. In fact, innovation often occurs without us thinking about it, in the form of sustaining innovation. We touched on more about the different types of innovation in Chapter 3.

## Pricing

One of the ways to generate more revenue is to increase prices. With that sentence, I feel like I've stated perhaps the most obvious business tip ever known, but it is remarkable how many businesses don't price their products or services effectively.

There are a number of ways that prices can be calculated, and many people try to overcomplicate the various pricing models. For me, they largely come down to:

- **market-led:** based on what the competition are charging;
- **cost-plus:** based on the cost of producing the product or service, plus a profit element;
- **value-based:** tied to the value that the end customer receives;
- **demand-based:** based on the demand for the product or service;
- **desire-based:** tied to the emotions that can be driven in the customer.

The mistake that many businesses make is that they only consider one or two of the above methods, and usually it is the market-led pricing or the cost-plus pricing approaches that they choose.

Instead of settling for just one type of pricing, I would urge any business looking to grow to consider pricing from all angles – internally by looking at demand and the cost of production, and externally by looking at value, desire and the market. Together with a systemized approach to ensure consistency of pricing, the business should be able to charge what it is worth. There are also various theories around menu pricing, anchoring and other presentation methods that can help the positioning of the business's price points.

## Chapter 11 summary

In this chapter we have taken a very quick journey through the different growth models that businesses might use. We've looked at organic methods of growth, such as doing more of what works, together with models such as franchising and licensing, and strategic alliances. We've also looked briefly at the opportunities that acquisitions may bring to a business. Finally, we touched on some of the tactics that businesses might use to increase their market share and their revenue, from pricing through to diversification and innovation.

Before proceeding to the next chapter, you should:

1 Think about all of the action points within the chapter.

2 Download and review the Chapter 11 supplementary material from www.carlreader.com/bossit

3 Answer the following questions:

   o Which of the growth models appeared to be interesting to you? We have only covered the models in very brief detail, and there are a number of resources available to help you understand the options more fully. Make a note of the models that could work for your business and the next steps that you will take to learn more.

   _____

   _____

   _____

   _____

o Which of the tactics merit more consideration? Make a list of the tactics that you like the sound of and which you would like to learn more about. This will help you organize your further research and find the right information to help you decide which tactics to use.

_____

_____

_____

_____

o When looking to grow a business, it is important to learn from others who have 'been there and done it'. Do you know anyone who can help you specifically with your business growth? Perhaps they have worked in corporate sales or have built their own business. Maybe they run a marketing agency. Make a note of some people and commit to contacting them to ask for help.

_____

_____

_____

# 12

# Scaling 101 – The funding model

In this chapter you will:

- learn about the different methods to finance a scaling business;
- understand how businesses are valued;
- understand the metrics that investors and lenders look for in businesses;
- learn about the fundamental differences between the outlook of investors and lenders.

The second piece of the scaling jigsaw is making sure that you have the right funding model for growth. A business that already has a track record will be raising funds based on development so far. It will be able to prove some of the metrics which had previously been just ideas in a business plan, and will be able to demonstrate a level of revenue growth.

Once a business is trading, you will also be able to consider different types of investment. Startup businesses, at the initial stages, are fairly limited and can only really consider loans, pre-seed equity investment, and some limited other financial products such as equipment leases or invoice factoring. With a bit of traction, other methods of financing become available, helping open up the doors to accelerated growth.

In this chapter, we will expand on what you learned about raising funds in Chapter 5 and financial management in Chapter 9. If you find any of the topics here seem a little advanced, it may be worth going back and refreshing your memory on the key points raised in those chapters.

Also, a word of support. You might feel that your business isn't one for this kind of financing, and that's fine. Scaling comes in many forms, and part of the process of scaling a business is understanding all options on the table.

# Equity funding... ramped up!

To kick off this deeper dive into how businesses can be funded, we'll take a look into the mysterious world of equity funding first. We will be taking it beyond the stage of a friend or colleague investing in a brand-new business idea, and look at how equity funding can be used for growing a business.

Even if you might feel that you don't want to give up equity, or that you'd never be 'right' for venture capital, it will be very worthwhile understanding the basics for your own business education. You might find that you end up working with suppliers or customers who are on this path, and it will help you understand some of the decisions that they make in their business. It will also help you should you ever get approached by a financier – you will be able to understand some of the jargon!

**CASE STUDY**    Funding considerations – Amazon

In the early 2000s, and before I got involved in any business that had equity investment, I saw the traction that Amazon was getting and couldn't for the life of me work out why they didn't just simply increase their prices by 1 per cent. They would have still been very cheap and it would have transformed their profitability (at the time, the company was loss-making).

It only dawned on me after a conversation with a friend that despite Amazon being one of the bigger companies in the world, they would only do this once they had reached a point of market dominance – the risk of damaging their market share growth was greater than the cost of making losses to their investors.

This goes against all 'small business' advice of managing the unit-level economics and focusing on profitability in every part of their business – but for them, it could well have been the right decision.

Let's look at the different stages of equity funding, together with the typical amounts invested and the valuations at that stage.

> **Important note:** There are two types of valuation numbers used – 'pre-money' and 'post-money'. Simply, pre-money is the company value before the investment, and post-money is after the investment. Company valuations in the equity investment world are notoriously difficult to establish, given that the equity investment is largely based on future potential rather than historic performance. We will talk more about company valuations later in this chapter. I've also used US dollars below, as the venture capital industry is largely centred in the US; however, your business will be valued in the jurisdiction that you and your funders are in.

## Pre-seed funding

*Usual funding amount – $5,000 to $200,000*
*No company valuation at this stage*

This can also be known as the bootstrapping stage, and it is typically funded by the founder or very close friends or family (sometimes known as a 'friends and family round'). This stage would normally encompass the testing and the feasibility studies, and the design of any product. During this stage, you would typically look to work with what you've got, and really test as much as you can to ensure that you can go into further funding rounds with confidence. The funding levels at this stage tend to be five-figure sums, and the business will be focusing on operating on as little cost as possible while building a proposition that can attract further funding down the line. Any legal agreements, which *should* be done properly even at this early stage, are nonetheless often done informally, due to the nature of the relationship between the entrepreneur and the investor.

## Seed funding

*Usual funding amount – $100,000 to $2 million*
*Company valuation – up to $5 million post-money*

This is where things get real! The business would be expected to launch its product or service at this stage, and to build traction (whether or not revenue results from this). Entrepreneurs would also be expected to start to recruit a team, and to go from an idea and a plan to action. Seed funding is normally attracted from angel investors, crowdfunding, and possibly from either friends and family as an extension of their investment, or smaller private equity houses. At this stage, investors may look for more complex mechanisms for their investment, such as convertible notes, which we will discuss later, and will also look for more robust legal agreements than might have been in place at the pre-seed funding stage.

## Series A

*Usual funding amount – $2 million to $15 million*
*Company valuation – $10 million to $30 million*

This is the first round of venture capital, and at this point a business would have a working business model, a strong team, and most importantly a scalable model. It isn't just about a 'great idea', which might have been sufficient in previous rounds. Investors would expect to see a strong strategy and a track record of growth (although not necessarily profitability). This round of investment would normally be the first round that venture capitalists would consider being involved in, but you might also find that previous investors seek to invest more by way of a 'follow-on' investment. Despite there being a number of investors, typically there will be one investor who will take the role of 'lead investor', and it is likely that they will take a seat on the board.

## Series B

*Usual funding amount – $15 million to $30 million*
*Company valuation – $30 million to $60 million*

Next up is the imaginatively titled Series B! The main difference here between Series A and Series B is that, normally, the round will be restricted to venture capitalists, solely due to the value of the investment. This round focuses on scaling up and increasing market share, with a focus on rapid growth towards the end goal of sale or IPO (initial purchase offering). At this stage, the investors involved will likely specialize in later-stage investments.

## Series C (and beyond)

*Usual funding amount – > $30 million*
*Company valuation – > $100 million*

While the traditional definitions focus on Series A, B and C, I will keep this section generic and focus on 'C onwards', covering any round between now and the IPO. At this stage, the funding is primarily used for building the company to a 'global' standard and will be used for building new products, entering new markets, and potentially even growth by large acquisitions. At this stage, the investment is far less risky and investors might include institutions such as hedge funds. Valuations at this stage are also far less subjective, as they can be based on hard data – companies at this stage would be expected to have strong revenue streams, reliable statistics on metrics such as customer churn, and proven histories of growth.

> **Important note**: While these are the generally accepted terms used in the investment marketplace, some of the values and stages might differ, as every business is different. For example, a business might need 'top-up' funding to reach the next stage, or might decide that seed or Series A funding is sufficient. Also, the typical value of deals and the valuations on the businesses can differ from country to country, and will also differ due to market sentiment.

# Other funding methods

Equity finance isn't the only option that growth businesses use to fund their development. There are a number of different options open to businesses, many of which we covered in Chapter 5. At this stage of a business, however, there are other options that are available to you, which can either be used in isolation or alongside other funding methods.

## *Crowdfunding*

Popular at a seed fundraising stage, crowdfunding can take place as either a rewards-based or equity-based offering, allowing private individuals as well as institutional investors to get involved early on in a business's journey. Recently, innovation has been focused around equity-based crowdfunding, and the platforms which facilitate these investments have built secondary markets for investors to sell off their shares. While the success stories from crowdfunding have been remarkable, it isn't as simple as building a pitch and uploading it. Businesses have to attract a substantial percentage of the investment outside of the platform and also have to rely a little on luck – things such as celebrity investment tend to help encourage the community to invest. Typically, a platform is paid a success fee for investment, and they act as a nominee shareholder for the other investors who may have invested a very small amount.

## Convertible notes

A convertible note is a form of short-term debt which converts to equity, usually at the point of the next financing round. Usually the note will entitle the investor to interest and a discount on the future valuation (so, for example, a 20 per cent discount would mean that an investor would receive the shares for $8 on conversion, if the other investors at the round receive them for $10). It is often used to bridge the gap between a current shortfall and a future investment round and has the benefit of the valuation not having to be determined at the point of issuing the debt – instead, by its nature, the valuation is based on the agreed valuation at conversion. There are two other things that need to be considered by a founder considering the use of convertible notes – they will often have a maturity date at which point the debt needs to be repaid if not converted, and some investors will push for a 'valuation cap', which will limit the price that they pay if the company takes off between the issue of the note and the next round of finance.

## Mezzanine finance

Another form of debt, mezzanine finance is typically used to bridge the gap between the debt finance and equity finance available. It is usually only used when there is a shortfall on the investment required, as it is very expensive to the business and high risk for the lender, with interest rates typically being 12–20 per cent per year. The risk for the lender is due to the fact that the debt is lower priority than any standard debt. This form of debt is only usually used for acquisitions or other specific projects.

---

### A moment to reflect

It is easy to get consumed by the jargon and obsess over the finer details of financing. When looking at raising finance, you should consider your overall appetite for debt and equity funding, and take advice from specialists regarding the nuances of each deal. There are some general descriptions here, but the devil is in the detail – and your best bet is to get someone with experience of these transactions to look at the particular agreement in front of you to make sure that it is what you are expecting.

---

## What does the investor get back?

The simple answer to this question is: a slice of the business! But as you've no doubt discovered, nothing in business is quite that simple.

The different stages of investment have different risk profiles, which in turn lead to different returns and motivations for the investors. For example, a Series C investor would only expect to double their money as it is relatively risk-free, compared with a seed investor, who might expect to make significantly more if the business is a success.

Investors at seed stage onwards would typically invest in a formal and professional manner, and both sides would be expected to take legal advice. There are a couple of things that these investors would want to be covered within any deal structure:

**Preference shares/preferred stock:** there are two general types of shares in a company – ordinary (sometimes referred to as common stock) and preference. The difference between these shares is included within the legal documents of the company; generally it entitles the preference shareholders to receive payment first in the event of winding up, and also to receive 'preferential' treatment (as decided between the shareholders) for the distribution of dividends.

Control: often, an investor might negotiate a different level of control than might be implied by the proportion of shares held. This is something that can trip up business owners who might have held onto a belief of needing 51 per cent of shares 'to keep control'. The reality for equity-funded businesses is that the balance of power will be decided in the shareholder agreement. Combined with the note on preference shares above, this is a useful time to highlight that while shares might appear equal on the face of it, the reality of the agreements might demonstrate that they differ in respect of payments due, ownership of the company, and voting rights. This is where strong legal advice is needed!

Vesting of shares: something that is usually introduced during the seed or Series A funding rounds is the vesting clause, which is intended to tie in the founders and any equity-holding employees to the business. The terms are agreed between the founder and the investor, but they typically involve the founder benefitting from the shares over time, based on either time served or (less commonly) on a performance basis. While this might seem unfair, it can be important to prevent a sticky situation arising from a co-founding arrangement, as this clause will stop a colleague leaving the business with their entire shareholding. The terms of the vesting would be a matter for negotiation.

Option pool: the final thing that investors would expect from a deal is an option pool, so that share options can be granted to key employees. These shares would likely have a similar vesting structure to that of the founder, so that all key personnel are aligned with the targets and interests of the company.

---

**A moment to reflect**

Reading through the above, you will probably see that attracting equity investment for growth can lead to the business being outside of your control. The clauses in the shareholder agreements, and the dilution of your shares, mean that it's entirely possible for you to become a cog within your own machine. It is no coincidence that very few founders remain in the business that they have started once they go down this path, and become 'relieved of their duties'. Make sure that, before you go down this path, you are comfortable with all that it can entail. It's not just a case of sacrificing today's pay cheque for tomorrow's exit valuation.

---

# What do investors and lenders look for?

While there are differences between bank funding and equity investors, both need to see a strong strategy, a robust plan, and the reassurance of an entrepreneur that they believe in. It also goes without saying that they will take a view on the industry that the business operates in and the current market conditions.

Normally, banks tend to look for the lowest-risk businesses to lend to, so will expect to see the following:

- reassuring levels of growth in the business, without being too aggressive;
- sufficient 'interest cover' (the ratio of earnings before interest and tax – EBIT – divided by interest);
- sufficient cash flow to afford the repayments through serviceability calculations.

---

## A moment to reflect

Remember my assumptions about Amazon in the early 2000s? A traditional bank lender would have the same mindset as I had. For the banks, the ability to repay debt is their key concern, over and above your growth as a business. If your growth will not also result in profits and free cash flow, bank lending will not be right for your business.

---

Equity investors will look for different things when appraising a deal. The stage of investment will dictate how reliable the statistics are, but generally they will be looking for evidence of growth, control of CAC (customer acquisition cost), continual increase of ARR (annual recurring revenue), a high LTV (lifetime value) per customer, and a low churn rate if you are in a business that retains customers over a period of time. Add in some more abbreviations such as TAM (total addressable market) and they will gauge the ability of your business to grow to a point that will give them the required level of return that they need, at the stage that they are investing in.

The reason that they need to do this is simple – there is such a high rate of failure, particularly early on in the game. To balance that out, they need to have a diversified portfolio with a number of potential high-return investments. According to a Techcrunch[1] survey, only around 40 per cent who close a seed or angel investment round actually get to Series A, with just over half of those getting to Series B after that.

# The thorny issue of valuations

So now, as we come towards the end of this chapter, we will take a look at valuations. These are ultimately the key issue in equity funding, and also the 'big pay cheque' once a business is sold or floated through an IPO (initial public offering).

One common business saying is that 'valuation is an art, not a science', and it's true to some extent. There are a number of ways of valuing a business, and often the value is reached through combining a number of these approaches and then finding either an investor or a buyer who agrees with that number! However, it's not just guesswork – the values that are then considered and compared are calculated through scientific methods, based on proven data within the business.

Some of the methods used to pull together a value are:

**Asset-based valuation** – this is effectively the value of the company's balance sheet: what it owns less what it owes. It takes no account of the value of the ongoing trade and is often referred to as the 'break up' or 'liquidation' value.

**Discounted cash flow (DCF) value** – this is a method of establishing the current value of future cash flows within the business. Think about it this way: imagine you had a choice of receiving £1,000 today, or £100 a month over the next 12 months. While on paper the monthly payment might seem better as it is a higher number, there are a few factors that you need to think about. Primarily, there is the risk that you might not receive all payments, and also that the value of £100 in a year's time is less because of inflation. The DCF calculations attempt to take the reduction in value over time into account, by discounting the future cash flows.

**Earnings multiple** – this is a way of estimating the value of future profits by multiplying an average year profit by a P/E (price vs earnings) ratio. This is effectively another way of estimating what the future cash flows of the business may be worth.

**Revenue multiple** – in some industries, you can estimate the value of a business by applying a multiple to the business's revenue. Again, this is a best guess at what the future value of the investment is, and is typically used in service industries where 'fee blocks' can be added to an existing business with a predictable set of costs attached.

**Market valuation** – where there are reliable comparables, such as in a franchise network or similar sales with publicly available information, a market-based valuation might be used. This is normally only used as a sanity-check against other methods.

**First Chicago/venture capital method** – this is a model used by investors in growth companies where there is little data. A valuation is performed on best-case, average, and worst-case scenarios, taking into account exit valuations and the discounted future value of investment return. The investor then applies a probability to each scenario to create a weighted average valuation.

**Dividend discount model** – this is a very basic model, taking into account the value of dividends over a period of time to calculate investor yield. This is typically used for very mature, stable companies that have already scaled.

---

## Chapter 12 summary

In this chapter we have taken a very quick journey through the different funding models that a business may use. As we had already considered basic lending options in Chapter 5, we focused more on equity funding and the stages that businesses can go through from startup through to their eventual stock market flotation or exit. We've looked at the different ways that businesses are valued, and we've also looked at some other forms of finance such as convertible notes, mezzanine funding, and crowdfunding.

Before proceeding to the next chapter, you should:

1 Think about all of the action points within the chapter.

2 Download and review the Chapter 12 supplementary material from www.carlreader.com/bossit

3  Answer the following questions:

o  What is your current appetite towards equity funding? Are you happy to forsake the control that a small business gives you in order to turn your business into a potentially global business? Use this time to note your initial thoughts on this and to set aside some time to explore what control means to you.

_____

_____

_____

_____

o  Which areas would you like to do more research on? We've covered a lot of ground in a short chapter, and some of the information might seem quite overwhelming. Make a note of any subjects that you would like to do some further reading on.

_____

_____

_____

o  If you are hoping to fund a scaling business, it is important that you pull together a strong team to help you with this. At the very least, this should comprise an accountant, a lawyer and a finance broker. Make a note of people in your own network that you should talk to, so that you can get recommendations. The accountants and lawyers that you have used so far might not be suitable, so think about the questions that you can ask them to ensure that they are up to the job and have the right experience and contacts for you.

_____

_____

_____

_____

# 13
# Scaling 101 – The staffing model

In this chapter you will:

- understand how to effectively recruit into a growing team;
- understand what you should look for in new team members;
- learn about how to bring together the team into an organization that works.

The third piece of the scaling jigsaw is making sure that you have the right staffing model for growth. For me, people are the most rewarding part of any business, but can also be the most challenging. Whereas funding a business is fairly scientific and data-led, us humans are complex beings and there is no 'rulebook' that dictates the one true way that a great team can be built. In fact, pretty much every war story that I could share about my experiences would come down to people: choosing the wrong ones, losing the great ones – and everything in between.

## Why do businesses get staffing so wrong?

Picture the scene. Your order book is full, and you are working 18-hour days. In fact, you're turning away customers! Forget worrying about having 'more month than money'… time is your most precious resource right now. You've missed a couple of family activities and have called in every favour possible to help out with school runs, deliveries, and the last-minute things that are normally in hand.

It is often this kind of tension that leads a business to need to recruit, and guess what? Most tend to make the mistakes that I described in Chapter 9:

- hiring on skills rather than attitude;
- setting arbitrary standards;
- hiring quickly, firing slowly.

Why do they do this? Simply due to a lack of planning. A surprising number of businesses don't plan their recruitment beyond knowing that they need an extra pair of hands. In fact, the fictional scenario described above is bound to be a direct result of a lack of planning and foresight, yet it is so relatable to many in business.

## A moment to reflect

This is a common theme across every part of a business, isn't it? A lack of planning is what tends to cause cash flow difficulties, staffing difficulties, operational issues and so much more. While most parts of the business can have a 'logical' fix, staffing challenges can be so much more complex – we're dealing with humans rather than numbers on a spreadsheet or products on a shelf. In the meantime, just remember that the Dream – Plan – Do – Review principle applies throughout the business, and throughout the life of the business!

We've touched on the fact that the results of getting it wrong are bad, but it is important to remember that the cost of a bad recruit isn't just the agency fees (sometimes up to 30 per cent of a team member's annual salary). One bad employment decision can impact the whole team, particularly if the problem is around cultural fit. The true cost of getting this wrong can be far greater than any sum of money that you spend on the wrong employee.

# Planning recruitment

We know what bad recruitment looks like, and we know that it isn't a good thing. It's also pretty clear that planning can help prevent bad recruitment, as it gives us time to make decisions and removes the urgency from the recruitment process. Much as we would build a warehouse before ordering stock, we should take on staff before the point at which we need them.

This is fairly simple to understand, of course, but it is actually a lot trickier to carry out. After all, recruiting a new team member can be like working out when to have a child – there may never be the 'perfect' time, until you look back with hindsight.

## Step 1: Plan for the financial impact

Using the parenting analogy, many potential parents fear the financial impact of having a child. It is exactly the same for recruitment, but the key thing to remember is that there's a far greater financial impact of limiting your business by *not* recruiting! Make sure that your financial projections include sufficient allowance for employing team members at the right point in the business (see Step 2).

## Step 2: Understand when you need the staff

Often, it's before you think you do! We can never guess exactly what point a business will need a new team member until there is a predictable pattern of employment vs performance – this being one of the main benefits of a scaling business with strong reporting. Until we get to that stage, it's wise to set some rule-of-thumb targets, which can give you an indicator to consider the need for additional staff. This could be as simple as a set number of customers per day, or a turnover figure. It might even be the number of hours that you as the business owner are working.

## Step 3: Create your recruitment plan

You might feel like you are too small to have an organization chart, let alone the backing documents that go with it, but please trust me – going through the process of creating a plan for your business's recruitment, much like every other planning process, will help you immensely. We'll look at how to do this in the next section.

---

### A moment to reflect

It's not about the plan – it's about the *process of preparing* the plan. This applies to financial planning, recruitment planning – in fact, any form of planning that you undertake in your business. The end product isn't the written plan; instead, it is the improvement of your thinking after you have undergone the process of creating the plan for your business. You will see things in a different light, you will consider recruits that you might not have even thought about, and you might find that you can combine/split roles. Whatever the outcome, it's the process of consideration that will really help you and the business.

---

# Creating your recruitment plan

For a recruitment plan to come together, you should start with the end in mind.

## Step A: The organization chart

The first thing that you should do is produce an organization chart of how your business would look if you had every position that your business might need. Don't worry if you don't have the staff just yet, or the ability to take on the staff; what we're trying to do here is understand the key functions in the business. Your organization chart might look like a traditional hierarchical chart, or you might decide to have a 'matrix' style chart with several lines of reporting. Some organizations even have spherical charts! Whichever way you decide to go with this, make sure that you map out the potential roles that you may have in your business. Table 13.1 provides an example of the more senior roles that might be in your business.

You can probably see here that the roles within the first three tiers of this organization might seem like overkill for a new or growing business, and that's fine. Our job here is to list out what the perfect business would look like for our industry, regardless of cost constraints.

---

## A moment to reflect

This process is designed to help you understand how the business should look, and later on we'll look at how to bridge the gap between now and the future. In the meantime, you should refer back to your systems, processes and procedures, to make sure that you have every essential system in your business covered through the organization chart. This might seem obvious – and on paper, it is – but the reality is that most dysfunctional organizations are that way because their organizational structure does not line up with the reality of how their business operates.

---

**Table 13.1** Example senior roles in an organization chart

| Tier | Job Title |
|---|---|
| 1 | Chief Executive Officer/Managing Director |
| 2 | Operations Director, Business Development Director, Finance Director, etc |
| 3 | Operations Manager, Sales Manager, Marketing Manager, Finance Controller, etc |

## Step B: Create the 'job descriptions' for each role

Next up, you need to create a comprehensive job description for each role. Yes – I know you don't have the money or the office space for them all to be employed just yet! At this stage, we're still planning a hypothetical model that can then be used to plan immediate and longer-term hires. On that basis, this isn't the time for being too creative with the format. I appreciate that a boring job description doesn't work too well for recruitment and am a big believer in making sure that they are tweaked when actually used. At this stage, though, we need the descriptions to be as clear as possible for internal use.

An effective job description at this stage would always include the following:

**A clear job title** – rather than being fancy, make sure that the job 'does what it says on the tin'. You'll have time to dream up crazy job titles later, if you want to, but at this stage it is important to have a very clear view of what the role requires. If one of the roles is for a credit controller, give them the job title of 'credit controller'. Trying to remember what a 'revenue management specialist' is will only hinder this whole process!

**List of responsibilities** – very simply, what does this role entail? List out the individual activities that the team member would be expected to do.

**Qualifications and experience** – list out the essential and desirable attributes of any recruit. Really think about this – does the role *need* someone with a degree? Do you *need* someone with ten years' experience in that particular software – or are you confident enough to train the right person?

**Reporting** – who does this role report into, and who reports into them? Make sure that this marries up with the organization chart and doesn't conflict with any systems or processes that you have in place. Also, think about any potential conflicts – you might find that some responsibilities sit better in another job description. In a traditional organization structure, you ideally want the reporting structures to be as clear as possible, and to reduce crossover of management.

**Key performance indicators** – what constitutes success for this role? List the concrete signs that will show the person in this role is successful, and who is responsible for managing those targets.

## Step C: Put the dream team together

So far, this might all seem like a lot of work for a small organization if you haven't been scaling yet, but here is where the magic happens. If the above steps have been followed, you will have a job description for each space in the organization chart, and you will be able to allocate names to the individual roles. Please note that you will almost certainly have people fulfilling several roles – you also will almost certainly have gaps! These are your future hires.

Before phoning your local recruitment agency to line up interviews for HR directors and other roles that might not be needed just yet, you then need to weigh up the following questions:

- What is the urgency of filling this role? Can it wait until we hit a certain point?

- Is anything being held up by this role not being recruited immediately?

- Do the roles need to be full-time, part-time, or just included within someone else's remit?

- Can someone else assume responsibility for another role today?

- Can someone else in the business be trained to do this job alongside their current role?

- Can this role be outsourced to an external agency?

By asking the above questions, you will find that you can sort the wheat from the chaff and focus on the important hires today to help your business remove any bottlenecks.

> ## A moment to reflect
>
> An organization chart should be as organic as the business that it is used within. It will evolve over time, and should never be considered finished. The same is true of job descriptions, and even who does what job in the business. Make sure that you are continually reviewing individuals against jobs against the organization chart – and the organization chart against the actual operations of the business.

# From dream team to reality

If you've gone through this exercise fully, you will see that you have gaps between the dream and where you are today. While you can add current names to new roles, you will also see where you need new blood – and often in a growing business, it will be 'on the tools'.

As our approach to recruitment is now planned, we can set about the process of finding new talent. Importantly, we'll be doing these things before the people are needed and before it becomes urgent.

Much like finding customers, finding staff involves elements of marketing and sales! We can break down the process as follows:

- creating an environment and the collateral to make employment at your business attractive;
- creating a process to successfully convert any potential recruits;
- finding new recruits and taking them through the process.

First up is the building stage. We have built very functional job descriptions for the purposes of understanding our organizational needs; but these are unlikely to be attractive to anyone considering a new role. After all, new employees will rightly ask 'what's in it for me'? No one really wants to sign up to a list of tasks and a process that they will be managed under.

We therefore need to make sure that we focus on why someone would want to become part of the business. We need to find ways to demonstrate our vision, values and culture. We'll go into more detail about how we create these in Chapter 14, the leadership model.

We also need to consider what staff benefits are on offer. Frederick Herzberg, in his theory of 'motivators and hygiene factors',[1] found that certain factors can lead to dissatisfaction (hygiene factors), whereas others can lead to satisfaction (motivators).

If we look at the kind of job description that we prepared from a functional perspective previously, this should in theory prevent dissatisfaction if done well. But let's be honest, we should be aiming for more than just 'no dissatisfaction'! So, we need to look at how we can include further facets to the jobs that we create, which can help encourage team members to be the best that they can be. The kind of things that we need to consider here are opportunities for achievement, recognition, responsibility and growth.

## A moment to reflect

This is a great opportunity to think back to the good and the bad in your employment history. Was there ever a job that you loved, despite the pay not being fantastic? A well-paid job that you couldn't get out of bed for? What was it about those jobs or companies that motivated or demotivated you? Think about how they did things and what you can do differently in your business, so that your team can embrace their role with the energy and enthusiasm that we all wish for.

While a well-written job description, complete with consideration of both hygiene factors and motivators, will help, in today's world you really should look to do a little more to help promote your brand as an employer. Some examples could include:

- testimonial videos from current team members;
- a website landing page about what it's like to work with you;
- features about staff members on your social media accounts;
- open days for potential employees to have some pizza and meet the team;
- activities outside of the 'day to day', such as running clubs and other social events;
- involvement with the local community and charities.

These things help, but it's important to keep it balanced. Some startups have copied the trends from Silicon Valley, loading their premises with ping pong tables and complementary bars. While these things are great on the face of it, people don't go to work and become engaged with their employer for these novelties. Culture goes far deeper than that, and we will briefly explore this in the next chapter.

## How do we take our workplace from theory to a team?

You've probably worked out through this whole book that I'm a big believer of getting things in place first, before taking action to drive it forward. After all, there is no point filling a leaky bucket! So, we'll start with building out what I believe is a good recruitment process, and then look at how you 'fill the funnel' with potential recruits.

One of the challenges in recruitment is the reliance on the interview. Often, when interviewing potential recruits, you get the best and the worst of them on the same day. They arrive early, highly groomed, and with some pre-prepared answers. They also are a bag of nerves, even underneath any interview bravado, and say what they think you want to hear!

Unlike some, I'm not one to say that the interview process is dead – far from it. I just believe that it can generally be done so much better. For me, common failings in the process include:

- current staff members making up the interview panel for roles that won't be in their team;
- inexperienced interviewers;
- lack of processes and set questions to remove personal bias;
- 'confrontational' interview processes;
- a focus on technical ability and experience, rather than personality and ambition.

We've already touched on the idea that we often hire on skills, but fire on attitude, and this hiring decision is usually supported by a traditional interview process. There's a whole lot to excellent recruitment and selection, and a ton of resources out there, so for now let's just highlight some of the things that I've learned along the way.

## Look beyond the CV

Often a CV or résumé can look very generic, and they are rarely helpful in the recruitment process (unless you are looking for arbitrary statistics such as educational achievements). Provided that someone hits the base criteria for the role, it is well worth doing some desk research beforehand. Look at their LinkedIn profile and other social media footprints to get a feel for the person behind the paper.

## Use pre-interviews as an interview

Before (and if) you meet face to face, why not use pre-interviews? These can be phone calls, video calls, or even a request for a team member to send a video answering a question or talking about a subject. If the role is customer-facing, this is a great way to see and hear how the interviewee presents themselves before making time for a face-to-face interview.

## Take the interview outside

Certainly for senior roles, I prefer to meet with potential recruits off site in a much more informal environment. Often, an interview at a pub or a café will reveal far more of the true person, as the environment will be much less intimidating than the office. What's more, it is never framed as an interview, just as an informal catchup. It works wonders!

## Think about the stages of your interviews

It is really important to get a second view on an employee, even if you use a systemized scorecard approach – we all have inherent bias towards certain things, and someone else will approach the interview with fresh eyes and a different perspective. I tend to prefer that team members get to meet their potential new colleagues, so a range of views can be considered before making the final decision.

## Remember the three key questions

The most important question to ask yourself is: 'Will they do the job?' Second: 'Will they fit in the team?' Bear in mind that these two questions are close in ranking – I only place the team one second as people can surprise me! Finally, and least importantly: 'Can they do the job?' There might be core skills needed at day one, but skills can always be taught. Attitude and personality can't!

## Consider using psychometric testing

There are a range of tools out there that can help you understand the motivations and personality types of potential recruits. You can use these to map potential recruits against the ideal for your business, the team that they will be in, or the role that they will fulfil.

Once you have worked out how you will conduct your interviews, it's time to get out there and start promoting! Over the past few years I have noticed the shift in the marketplace towards online recruitment – and it's not just through job sites. LinkedIn is probably the hottest place to recruit, as almost everyone in the B2B world is there. I also would supplement any job listings with adverts, sponsored social media posts, open days... in fact, we have gone as far as having hoardings at the local football grounds, flyers distributed, and billboards! You really do need to treat recruitment as another marketing activity of your business.

Another way is to consider using an agency, and for some industries this is simply the only way to access the best talent. There are some things to bear in mind, though:

- **Cost:** most agents charge a success fee, which is usually negotiable. It will still be a significant percentage of the annual salary, which you will need to factor in.

- **Clawback period:** if the recruit isn't right, there is a period (again negotiable) during which you will not need to pay the fee. Make sure that both you and the agent are clear on the terms of this.

- **First on the desk:** we have had an unfortunate dispute with an agent who sent us an unnamed CV – we didn't interview at the time, but then accepted the CV from another agent, and ended up having to pay both agents. Think about potential conflicts like this that might occur and consider how you could mitigate this. Are you happy to give an agency exclusivity over your recruitment?

- **Quality control:** this might sound brutal when it comes to people, but you need to ensure that your agency has some level of checking over who they put to you. Another agency pitched a candidate who it turns out had been convicted of fraud, for a role in a chartered accountancy business. Make sure that you understand what they will and won't offer as part of the selection process, and that you set out clearly what is expected of them.

# Managing the team

Once you have your team members on board, it is time to start thinking about that tricky thing – management. Perhaps the one thing that I wish someone had taught me early on is this:

> *Someone who is good at their job won't necessarily be good at managing others doing their job.*

Like most things in business, it is blindingly obvious when you see it written down, but we've all been there: working for a company managed by the person who has hung around the longest, or did the best at school 20 years ago. The reality is that managing is a skill in itself, and once your team hits that critical mass, you will need someone who is able to manage them appropriately.

The concept of management is also complicated by the misuse of 'manager' in many job titles! After all, there are process managers, finance managers, sales managers, facilities managers… many of whom don't manage anyone! For the purposes of this section, we will be looking solely at those who have a responsibility for managing people, rather than functions of the business.

In the next chapter, we will explore how to recruit and manage the managers (yes, even the best managers need managing)! In the meantime, let's take a look at the things that you, and in turn your managers, will need to think about when it comes to simply managing the team.

## Understanding the people

For me, the key to people management is understanding each and every person as an individual. Often, poor management is a result of a presumption that everyone is like us. It goes back to that often used saying: 'treat others how you would like to be treated'. Instead, try this alternative golden rule: 'treat others how they would like to be treated'. Make sure that you know who they are, what their motivations are, and what their aspirations are. This will help you understand how best to communicate and manage them.

## Set clear expectations

A common failing in many managers is that they abdicate tasks to their team, rather than delegating properly. When working with a team member, you need to make sure that you set the task, expectations and any guidance out clearly, and work with them to meet those objectives.

## Set a clear appraisal system

Appraisals might seem like a routine that we all blindly follow, but if they are done correctly, they can be hugely powerful. Make sure that you have a broad structure to performance management meetings, and that it isn't simply a case of both sides filling in check-box forms. Ultimately, the end result of every appraisal meeting should be a clear set of actions and goals for both sides.

## Make time for the human side

I don't suggest that managers should be best friends with their reports, but it is important that you get to know each other on a human level. Celebrate the wins, share mutual challenges, and start to understand where each of you is coming from. Building that bond with the team members can only help when the going gets tough.

# What happens if it all goes wrong?

At the start of this chapter, we touched on the areas where businesses get recruitment wrong. The cost of a bad hire goes far beyond that of their salary and any recruitment costs. A bad egg can really unsettle a team and disrupt the culture that you have built.

Recruitment mistakes do happen, though! You can know all this stuff logically but still make a bad decision or a rushed decision. Sometimes your intuition is wrong, and sometimes people change. If you get into the flow of recruiting people, you will no doubt have to have difficult conversations about ending relationships too.

The first thing to be aware of is that you need a process to identify when it is going wrong. If a team member isn't performing, it is likely that regardless of how strong your management is, their colleagues will have spotted the signs first. Provided that you can step in quickly, you will limit the damage to the other team members, who may well feel unmotivated if someone is seen to be getting away with not performing.

Poor performance isn't the only reason why businesses have to let staff members go. There is also the issue of conduct, and most employment legislation has provision for different types of misconduct, such as standard and gross misconduct.

Provided that the poor conduct or performance isn't so bad that it justifies immediate disciplinary processes, you should first have an informal chat with the employ to explain your concerns. For me, these conversations should be capped to a very short time limit and should be backed up with data (such as performance versus KPIs, or evidence of conduct). Importantly, you will need to also make a note of this conversation so that it can be used if required for any further disciplinary action. Usually, a quiet word in private is enough to motivate a staff member into performing better, but sometimes it isn't enough – in those circumstances, it's time to commence formal procedures, including performance management measures or disciplinary procedures. These are not matters to be taken lightly, so my strongest advice in this situation is to consult an expert to ensure that you stay on the right side of any employment legislation.

## Chapter 13 summary

In this chapter we have taken a very quick journey through the process of creating a staffing model. We kicked off with a reminder of the challenges that most businesses face when recruiting staff, usually through a lack of planning. We built out a 'dream' organization chart, together with job descriptions, so that we could match current staff members to the chart and identify gaps. Next, we talked briefly about the recruitment process, and the basics of managing a team.

Before proceeding to the next chapter, you should:

1  Think about all of the reflective questions within the chapter.

2  Download and review the Chapter 13 supplementary material from www.carlreader.com/bossit

3  Answer the following questions:

o  Employing lots of staff might seem a way off, but as we have seen in this chapter, the need for a team can come very quickly. When will you carve out time to prepare an organization chart for how your scaled business could look, together with the roles and responsibilities?

_____

_____

o  There will be areas in the senior team that you are unlikely to be able to cover yourself, but will need in a growing business. This might be a finance director, HR director, marketing director… in fact, any function within the business. The challenge with these roles is that they are expensive. Can any of them be outsourced? Make a note of where your larger business could benefit from some extra skills, but not on a full-time basis.

_____

_____

_____

○ We touched on some of the basics of management towards the end of this chapter. It's a notoriously difficult task, full of theories, but I tend to find that our experiences also shape how we manage. Make a note of some formative experiences that you've had with managers, good and bad, so that you can dwell on them and take any lessons to help you become a better manager.

---
---
---
---

# 14
# Scaling 101 – The leadership model

In this chapter you will:

- learn about leading a team;
- find out how to create a winning culture;
- understand how to build out multiple layers of management.

We've made it to the final part of the scaling jigsaw! The process for management was covered in the last chapter – but you know what? Someone must lead and manage the managers!

And for me, this is my favourite part of the process, as there is nowhere to hide.

Those who play sports will know what I mean. Let's take football as an example: you can be the best player on the pitch, but still lose the match. There are so many external circumstances that can affect the result – everything from how your teammates perform through to things like the weather and the referee. Leadership is not like that. The art of leadership is only impacted by your own performance. There is no one else to blame, no one else to prop you up, and it's perhaps the only one of the four facets of scaling a business that is not reliant on facts and figures.

## Building an unstoppable culture

You may have heard of the phrase 'culture eats strategy for breakfast'. On the face of it, that phrase might imply that culture is the only thing worth worrying about – I can assure you, it's not. Instead, the two go hand in hand. A business with a strong culture but no strategy will fall apart, as its culture will unwind without the structure of a solid strategy. Likewise, a business with a strong strategy but a poor culture will find that it is continually trying to drive forward with its feet on both the accelerator and the brake.

Before we ponder what a culture is, I think it's worth discussing what a culture isn't. There's a current trend of focusing on the tactics that businesses use as part of their cultural identity and confusing them with the culture itself. Businesses might cram their buildings with ping pong tables and allow team members to wear t-shirts, but these tactics won't go far in masking a culture that has evolved badly.

There is one way to build a great culture and the clue is in this sentence – it needs *building*. Rather than letting a culture develop, a culture should be created by design. Like many things in business and in life, it is much harder to change course once the rot has set in.

## Components of a winning culture

There are a number of theories around culture, and you can lose yourself for days reading about the finer details. For me, though, culture is made up of a few key elements (Figure 14.1).

We covered the vision back in Chapter 10. For the purposes of scaling so far, we have only needed to have clarity on where we are going for ourselves. When it comes to leadership and building an effective culture, though, this vision needs to permeate through the team. It needs to be the central point of the stories that define the business and the foundation underneath everyone who works

**Figure 14.1**   The elements of culture

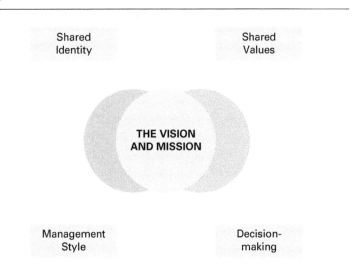

there. This is the thing that will get your employees out of bed and bringing their best each and every day.

From there, we have the four supporting elements that help keep the team on the right path.

## Shared identity

This is how the business looks and feels, internally and externally. There is no right answer as to what a 'good' identity is. The wrong answer comes when the identity is incongruent with the rest of the culture, the operations, and the central core vision. The identity can come from a number of angles. Does the business dress code stipulate formal dress or branded t-shirts? Does the team get actively involved in charitable and socially responsible activities? What colour are the walls in the office? Do you have an open-plan office or separate cubicles for the team to work in? Perhaps the greatest incongruency can arise when the external identity, such as logos and website, is the opposite of what actually goes on internally – this confuses the outside world and can demotivate the team.

## *Shared values*

This is all about how the business goes about its day-to-day activities. For a culture to thrive, the team needs to know what is and isn't acceptable; and perhaps more importantly, needs to live by the values in their dealings with all stakeholders. We will run through the process that I used to create the values in my team later in this chapter.

## *Management style*

It's all well and good having an organization chart, and people sitting in the role of management, but you need to consider how the managers manage! What level of responsibility will be passed on to the team? Will they be given authority as well as responsibility? Will you adopt a hierarchical or a flat management structure? Will you tolerate, or encourage, micromanagement in certain situations? What level and format of reporting will you expect? Will you adopt a formal, systemized approach to management?

## *Decision-making*

Finally, we have the impact of decision-making on the culture. Who really calls the shots? Is everything pushed up the chain to a bottleneck near the top of the organization chart (yes, I'm looking at you!)? Is decision-making performed by committee, holding up how the organization makes decisions? Or is the burden all on one person? If we are looking to empower teams, do decisions get delegated, or abdicated? If there is a board, how much input do they have in the decisions of the managers? Bringing this all together, who does the buck stop with?

---

**A moment to reflect**

Have a think about businesses that have inspired you in some way. It may have been your experience as a customer, or perhaps a previous company that you worked for or alongside. What was it that made the business stand out? Which cultural building blocks from the above model were evident? How can you use these in your own business?

---

# Creating a shared identity

To help put more meat on the bone of each of these components of culture, I would like to share my own experiences of building a culture within my business.

For us, identity was really difficult. We were competing in a service industry (accountancy) which had a pretty 'set' look of navy logos, formal dress and dull offices. At the time we set our identity, accounting firms would rarely go out of the office without the men wearing ties – and some would even go so far as demand that women wear skirts rather than trouser suits.

We did a lot of the things that many businesses now believe is all that is needed for culture: we had the branded polo shirts, colourful logo, colourful website, even the colourful office! We bought the pool table, the bean bags and the stereos.

Guess what happened? After the 'grand opening' of the freshly redecorated office, the team members reverted to their own norm!

We found the hard way that identity isn't just about a lick of paint and bright colours. It permeates all the way through what team members do and the way that they do it.

A great example would be a stereotypical tech startup company. Within five minutes, you are bound to hear the word 'super' used as a prefix, rather than on its own. You'll also see that the team are super-motivated, super-friendly...

In my experience, the identity has to come from the top of the organization. Teams naturally follow their leader and will look to mirror their acts, good and bad. By being the identity that you wish your team to be, some traits will be inherited. It's not just a case of buying some printed t-shirts and hoping for the best!

# Creating and using a shared set of values

We've touched on values already. I found that setting clear values provided us with an anchor against which we could consider anything in the business, but perhaps the trickiest part was working out what the firm's values should be!

All of us have personal values that we live by, and with a bit of time and a notebook, we can narrow down our personal values reasonably quickly. We know what we stand for as individuals: the things that we wouldn't expect from ourselves and the things that we would hope that others say about us.

If you were to do the same exercise with your life partner, you may well find that you have similar values. You may even have the same values, but with a different emphasis. It would be unusual, however, for you both to construct an *identical* value set, using the same wording and the same emphasis, unless you had discussed it before.

Therein lies the difficulty with creating values for a business. As a team, you will have a number of different personalities, with different backgrounds and experiences. Some will have had their personal values shaped through experiences, others through upbringing. The likelihood of everyone's values being completely aligned is near zero.

We approached this as collaboratively as possible, but some difficult decisions had to be made.

To begin with, we asked the team to scribble down as many values as they could that they felt were important to them and the business on individual sticky notes and put them up on the wall. Before long, we had an office full of yellow sticky notes, and you can imagine that at that point, the process seemed much tougher than we had first guessed!

Thankfully, some common themes evolved. First, several values were duplicated – for example, we had a lot of sticky notes with the word 'honesty' written on it. We also noticed that many of the words used were similar to others. Because of this, we tried to group similar values into batches. As an example of this, 'honesty', 'truth', and 'integrity' might have been in a similar batch. From there, we found that there were common themes, and between us we agreed on the headline value for each 'batch', with a lot of supporting words and phrases to help support that value.

Eventually we reached a set of values that we all agreed on for d&t: Professional, Caring, Passionate and Innovative.

So, we'd created the values – how did we use them?

I didn't want to do what most businesses did, which is to put the words up on our website and maybe put a sign up on a wall and then forget about them. We've seen how incongruence in identity can lead to confusion – the same thing can happen with values. Claiming one set of values and living by another is inherently wrong, and it's also bad business – I am a strong believer that values should be so much more than just part of your marketing collateral. To that end, we looked at how we could integrate our values into as much of what we do as possible. We talked about our values in team meetings and used them as an anchor if we had any dilemmas internally. We also weaved them into our processes. Here are some practical examples of what we did:

## Using them as part of a balanced scorecard for innovations

Rather than just weigh up innovations on a cost/benefit perspective, we wanted to make sure that any innovations that we undertook were true to our values and fulfilled our stakeholders (see

Chapter 10). Therefore, we assessed every innovation by the value that it helps us adhere to, and the stakeholder that it serves. This allowed us to ensure that we had a rounded perspective on any innovations that we looked to implement within the business.

### Using them as part of our management

From recruitment to staff appraisals, we use our values to anchor the behaviours that we expect from our team, and should there ever be an issue within the team, we can use our values as a 'guiding light'.

### Using them as part of our marketing

From our careers website through to printed flyers, we used our values as one of our key marketing messages, resulting in everyone who is a stakeholder in the business being fully aware of how we work and what to expect.

## Creating a management style

The next part of the culture model is the management style that permeates through the organization. We covered the basics of management in the last chapter, so I don't intend to repeat those points. Instead, let's focus on how we can systemize whatever way we choose to manage a business, so that it can grow beyond the current layers.

At the start of this chapter we touched on the acid test for scalability: whether a business can grow to multiple tiers of management. This is only possible by having processes for management, so that more senior managers can manage their reporting managers, and ensure that the role is being taken seriously and performed well.

First up is clarity on how the business will be managed. Much of this will be based on the organization chart, as there will be some obvious reporting lines. You will need to consider the impact of any matrix-style reporting situations, where an individual's targets will fall under the remit of two or more managers. By setting out the rules of the game for these situations, you will be able to avoid your management structure becoming farcical through confusion and internal politics.

Once you have this clarity of who is managed by whom, and who is responsible for each individual KPI and each individual team member, you can start thinking about some of the processes that you can put into place. These may include annual and periodic appraisals, feedback systems, 360 feedback on seniors, staff engagement surveys and so much more. There are software packages available to help you manage most of these processes.

These are some of the things that you need to think about for your management teams, and as you evolve to multiple tiers of management, each level will need to think of these:

## How much of their time will be devoted to managing?

This might sound obvious, but it is something that you need to consider when the business is growing. Often, a manager automatically inherits their position from their original job 'on the tools', and juggles both roles simultaneously – for example, managing the team while also doing the cleaning themselves. Without a discussion about their workload, it's likely that they will become a failure in either one of the two roles that they are taking on. Make sure that you set clear expectations and get their feedback on the available time to devote to each side of their role.

## What development training is needed?

As mentioned before, managing is a job in itself, and for me CPD (continuing professional development) is perhaps more important for managers than it is for the wider team. Make sure that you work with your managers to understand how they can improve, to better serve their reports and the business.

## What tools can help them manage more effectively?

While management is ultimately a human-to-human relationship, the end result of management is to improve the data within the business. Make sure that each manager has the ability to get data on both the team members and the KPIs that they are responsible for, so that they can decide the best way to manage based on facts rather than assumptions. Also, think about whether there are any tools that can help systemize the softer side of management – even a simple task list can help ensure that each team member feels valued and has a regular opportunity to give feedback to the organization.

# Creating a decision-making culture

The final piece of the culture model is around decision-making: not on an individual basis, but how the organization makes its decisions. We've already touched on some of the key issues – many organizations fall foul of abdication, upward delegation to someone more senior, or decision by committee. This is as a natural result of a fear-based culture. If team members don't feel safe to get things wrong sometimes, they will naturally look to pass the buck to someone else to save themselves.

Despite your best intentions as a leader, this kind of culture can easily creep into any business. Sometimes, it is entirely accidental – someone might have had a negative experience with a previous employer and starts acting in a way that others follow. Regardless of how it comes about, your job as a leader is to ensure that whatever vision you have for your culture is implemented throughout the business.

Most businesses now aspire to a culture where their team members are empowered to make decisions within their area of responsibility, and to own those decisions. If this is the route that you are looking to take, these are my suggestions:

## Set clear expectations with the team

Make sure that the team are fully clear on which areas they can and can't make decisions, and any limits. If you have, for example, a financial limit on decisions that a certain level can make, tell them! By giving clarity on the expectations, team members shouldn't be under any illusions as to what is and isn't acceptable from them.

## Adopt a coaching culture in the early days

Even if the team is clear on what they are and aren't allowed to do, they will likely feel nervous when it comes to making the first big decision. Make sure that they feel welcomed to ask questions and help them by facilitating the decision-making process. This is a very tough job, as it requires you to tread that fine balance between support and actually making the decision yourself. It is important that you pass back the decision-making to the team member whenever possible.

## Make the business a safe space

There will be mistakes along the way. People will make bad decisions and it will cost the business money. You need to accept that and appreciate that it is part of the process of delegating the decision-making. More importantly, you need to let the team know that you are catering for some errors in judgement along the way. By both communicating this and acting in the same way, you will help your team realize that they really are free to work autonomously.

### Resist the urge to step in

As a leader, perhaps the second worst thing that you can do is step back into a management role and make a decision for one of your team – this is only topped by overturning a decision that they have already made! In the final notes to the book, you will read more of my own experiences in this area. But in the meantime, just remember that the cost of doing this will almost certainly outweigh any benefit of making the decision – as tough as that seems at the time!

# Leading from the top

The way in which we conduct ourselves has a massive impact on our team, our customers, and everyone else that we work with in our business. Some of the most important things that I've learned along the way are noted below.

### Leadership is about setting the path, and then getting out of the way

This was a turn of phrase used by an executive chairman of a Silicon Valley tech company, during a conversation that I had with him. I asked him about how he had built such an outstanding culture that resonated through each and every team member of his (then) US$60 billion company. He made it seem so simple!

### Praise in public, work on challenges in private

This was a lesson that I learned from seeing the results of bad management of a colleague. When managing or leading, you don't need to assert your position publicly. Whenever possible, pass the praise on to someone else and assume responsibility for the challenges. If you then need to address those challenges with someone else, it is always best done behind closed doors.

### Employ those who are better than you

Perhaps this is obvious, but you need to make sure that you fill your team with people who are far better than you in their own areas. There is an old saying: don't have a dog and bark yourself. Find the right people for the job, learn from them daily and let them get on with it!

### Take a helicopter view whenever possible

As you go through the management and leadership journey, you will become more and more detached from what happens on the ground. Embrace this! Your view of the business will become more unique over time, and that can help add the most value to your managers and their teams. A fresh set of eyes can notice so many things.

### Ask why things can't be done ten times quicker or better

Even the best of us look for the easy answer sometimes. One of the simplest questions that you can ask is 'why'. Try to understand what the limiting factors are and challenge them. More importantly, ask why things can't be done with a dramatic improvement in outcome. This forces a different level of thinking – and often, limiting factors are shattered!

### Keep it simple, and don't be afraid to ask twice

Sometimes, you will be overwhelmed by the way that things are presented to you. Don't be afraid to ask for an explanation – you aren't expected to be the cleverest in the room! A tool I like to use is to ask for things to be explained in language that an eight-year-old can understand. If a concept cannot be explained so simply, it is possible that the team member is confused themselves.

## Take advice

While you might naturally be the top of the organization, it is highly unlikely that you are the best at everything. Sometimes we develop an air of invincibility about ourselves, and there is only one way out from that… Make sure that you remain grounded and realistic about what you can do, and don't be afraid to take advice from those who have been there and those who are experts in the things that you aren't.

## Don't be too close, but don't be too far

This one is a really tricky balance to get right, and the nature of your relationships with the team changes over time. You have to try to strike the balance of being approachable, supportive and helpful, without being 'best friends' with everyone. As your organization grows, an unfortunate side effect is that you won't know everyone in the business. Try not to be the awkward boss! Instead, as the business develops, build strong professional relationships with your management team, and allow them to do the same with their teams.

## Learn to wear other hats

As a leader of an organization, your role is to find the right paths that provide the most satisfaction to as many stakeholders as possible. Perfection is almost impossible and, instead, you have to learn the art of compromise. Wearing other hats in a decision-making process is a great way to help you and your team understand the viewpoints of others and create effective answers.

## Take a balanced view

The business rollercoaster can really hit us at times. Just remember: it's rarely as good as it seems, nor as bad as it seems.

## Chapter 14 summary

In this chapter we have taken a very quick journey through the process of creating a strong culture in your business. We have looked at my cultural model, comprising five key elements: the shared identity, the shared values, the management style, and the decision-making style, all underpinned by the stories we use, which is based on the vision of the business. I've also shared some of my key learnings along the way and things that I wished that someone else had told me!

Before proceeding to the next chapter, you should:

1   Think about all of the reflective questions within the chapter.

2   Download and review the Chapter 14 supplementary material from www.carlreader.com/bossit

3   Answer the following questions:

o   Designing a culture for your business is essential, otherwise it will be designed for you. I know from my own experiences just how hard it is to 'retrofit' a culture into a business that has already developed a personality of its own. On that basis, please commit to a date to explore this more fully and start the process of creating a culture by design.

_____

_____

o   We spent a lot of time exploring the value of building a strong set of values and processes for management. Both tasks are very different, but both also require some planning. Make some notes about how you intend to create your values with your team and how the process can work. Also, make some notes about any systems that you feel you need to put into place to help with systemizing your management process, such as online HR services, staff engagement surveys, or a fixed appraisal process.

_____

_____

_____

_____

_____

o  My leadership notes at the end of the chapter are just the things that have resonated with me along the way. You will no doubt have your own quotes or ways of doing things. The main thing for adopting these practices is to ensure that they become part of what you do as a leader, each and every day. If there are any other things that you live by, make a note of them now, and think about how you can make sure that you live by them consistently rather than just when you remember to.

_____

_____

_____

_____

# 15
# Final words of advice

If you've read this book all the way through, chances are you're at the beginning of your business journey. Winding up, retiring and the end (or next phase) of your business journey may well be the furthest thing from your mind – but it's an important part to consider about being your own boss.

So, now that we've been through all the steps of starting, building and running your business, I want to share with you a bit of this article I wrote in November 2018. At the time, I was moving from an active CEO role into a more supportive joint chairman role – essentially, stepping away from the day-to-day running of my business.

## From CEO to chair[1]

I often write about things that I feel I can help business owners with. But today, I'm writing about what me and my business partner Ben are learning about as we move into the joint-chairman role – each and every day, on the job.

### The biggest change in my business life

We all have *that* dream. To build a business, kick back, and retire on a beach somewhere. To let others take what we've built and push it forward.

I'm partway on that journey, and I'd like to share the good, the bad, and the ugly of the situation.

Over the past few years at #TeamDT, we've built a management team, and then the processes to help the managers have a way of managing. The wrong way round, but it worked eventually. We had the people and gave them the tools for their jobs.

This limited us, as management only takes you so far. So, we've been on the journey of building a leadership team. Finding people who are better than me and Ben, to take on our executive responsibilities and take what we've done to the next level.

**Making yourself redundant is far more difficult than it sounds!**

On the face of it, it should be easy. Give someone else your chair and desk (I did that a couple of years ago). Tell them what to do. And get out the way.

The challenge is that to be a truly effective CEO/MD/head of an organization, as Ben and I are used to being, you need to make decisions quickly, roll your sleeves up, and get on with it. In truth, that's what we enjoyed doing too. That's the buzz of being in business.

To be a truly effective chair, you need to help facilitate your board. You need to help them identify their and the business's opportunities and weaknesses. You need to help develop their thinking and act as a sounding board rather than as a solution.

For someone who is used to creating, deciding, and doing – this is a *real* culture shock!

For the wider team who may be used to asking you for answers – it's even tougher.

**What advice can I give to anyone else looking to make this move?**

I normally only give advice on things that are tried and tested, usually by me. So, I'm going to caveat this advice by saying that it is based solely on my learnings to date, and we're still going through this process.

But, that said, this is what I have learned so far:

**You need to get over yourself to do this properly.** Most of us who have built a business to any real level will undoubtedly have a large ego. To make the transition to chair, you need to first acknowledge the ego, and then get over it.

**You need to respect the decisions of your board and your team.** If you undermine them in any way – by either making decisions for them, complaining about their decisions, or contradicting their decisions – you end up taking one step forward and five steps back. While you might not agree with their tactical decisions, you need to weigh up whether the cost of undermining the board outweighs the risk to the business of that decision. Bearing in mind you'll be investing a significant sum in salaries, team development, and the sheer effort in managing the organization-wide change to allow this, it has to be a 'million-pound risk' to even be worth undermining. Bearing in mind that our team, our clients, the community, our market, and being blunt – my family – depend on the right tactics being implemented, it is a difficult balance at times, but an important one.

**Your job is to serve the board.** The board will have different requirements from you, depending on their needs. Being a sounding board is key, but you might need to fill in with functional roles. For example, I still work crazy hours as an 'evangelist' (or as I prefer, a flag waver). Ben still works crazy hours in transitioning all of the operational expertise and experience to the team. But we have to accept that we are now servants of the board – and when they tell us what we are or aren't needed for, we need to listen.

**You have to create even more distance.** One of the toughest things about growing a business is that you lose touch with the team. At 20 staff, I knew the names of everyone's partners, pets, etc... this became tougher and tougher, hence the need to build a management team. Now, rather than distance being a factor created by scale, it has to be a factor created by design. If I allow any long-serving team member to come directly to me rather than follow the structure set by the board and the management team, I unwind all of their good work. If I allow any customer or supplier to negotiate directly with me, I risk jeopardizing not only the processes but also the culture that the team are trying to set. I have to deliberately make myself impotent insofar as how the business runs, so that the business can run.

**Your work isn't over.** Instead, I've found myself focused even further into the future: looking at the next 20–30 years rather than the next few months; looking at the wider changes that might impact the business; creating relationships outside of our customers and prospects; and helping to find the seeds for my board to plant, so that #TeamDT can continue to flourish.

As you can see, business, and indeed life, is a work in progress. This article was written just three months before my new role of co-chair became official, and at that point the tools were put down.

Maybe you're not quite there yet, but most of us at some point in our working lives think of retirement. We daydream of sitting on a beach, sipping cocktails, listening to our own choice of music and no one else batting an eyelid. We might dream of taking up new hobbies, indulging in a fitness regime that we never had time for before, or travelling the world.

The reality is that I just happen to enjoy business.

I might have been able to go through the journey of growing and scaling, but the end point is a poor anti-climax. I'm not ready to retire just yet!

Since becoming co-chair of the board at d&t, I've had the opportunity to do some amazing things. I've become involved in taking over the running of a National League South football club, and worked with some huge brands such as American Express and Mercedes Benz Vans, to help them target the small business market through some joint thought leadership and small business advocacy. I started a podcast which hit 18th in the global charts and became 'New and Noteworthy'. I've continued my media work, being on both national TV and radio, I've travelled globally as a speaker, and continue to share my journey, warts and all, on my social media channels.

But do you know what I love the most?

Getting stuck into the business when I'm asked to. Because that is what drives me.

Thinking of creative new ideas to help our marketing team. Brainstorming solutions to tricky problems. Helping to look at things with fresh eyes, away from the day-to-day grind. Perhaps most importantly, being there for my board, who have afforded me the time to do some amazing things, such as writing this book.

It has not come without its challenges. Becoming a couch potato has been far too tempting, and I'm almost certain that the lack of day-to-day contact with people outside my house has not helped my own sense of wellbeing.

After all of the steps and practical advice in this book, I wanted to leave you with a reminder that you can do it – you *can* reach those dreams of early retirement – but make sure you think about what's next. Is retirement what you really want? Is building a business what you really want?

Life is a journey, and it's madness to try to reach an 'end'. It's far better to enjoy the process.

Whatever it is that you want: if you dream it, make a plan, take action and keep reviewing progress – you can probably get there. BOSS IT!

# NOTES

## Introduction

**1** Department for Business, Energy and Industrial Strategy, https://assets. publishing.service.gov.uk/government/uploads/system/uploads/ attachment_data/file/852919/Business_Population_Estimates_for_ the_UK_ and_regions_-_2019_Statistical_Release.pdf (archived at https://perma.cc/XN8X-JQXB)

## Chapter 1

**1** City AM: Why most businesses never reach £1m turnover: https:// www.cityam.com/why-most-businesses-never-reach-1m-turnover/ (archived at https://perma.cc/98MN-NRLP)

**2** Maslow, AH (1943) A theory of human motivation, *Psychological Review*, 50 (4), 370–96, https://doi.org/10.1037/h0054346 (archived at https://perma.cc/E54U-7YNM)

**3** Maslow, AH (1987) *Motivation and Personality*, Harper & Row, New York

**4** World Options survey (August 2017), https://uk.worldoptions.com/ download_file/view_inline/263 (archived at https://perma.cc/R3AS-5NXC)

**5** https://keap.com/business-success-blog/business-management/small-business-owner-profiles-2 (archived at https://perma.cc/638F-K9VF)

**6** Longitudinal Small Business Survey, BEIS (July 2017), https://www.gov. uk/government/statistics/small-business-survey-2017-businesses-with-employees (archived at https://perma.cc/W7AX-K7YE)

**7** Gerber, ME (2009) *The E-Myth Revisited: Why most small businesses don't work and what to do about it*, Harper Collins, New York

# Chapter 2

**1** Paul J Meyer, www.pauljmeyer.com (archived at https://perma.cc/9CKA-GN3V)

# Chapter 3

**1** http://www.tesla.com/en_GB/about (archived at https://perma.cc/3BQ3-3XRG), 29 October 2017

**2** https://www.forbes.com/sites/jlim/2015/05/07/canva-carries-out-7-year-vision-to-disrupt-digital-design/ (archived at https://perma.cc/QD6M-Y8MX)

**3** https://about.canva.com/story/ (archived at https://perma.cc/UNV3-KLVU)

**4** https://about.canva.com/story/ (archived at https://perma.cc/UNV3-KLVU)

**5** https://about.nike.com/ (archived at https://perma.cc/W4P4-RZES)

**6** https://www.academia.edu/7078862/Nike_a_case_study_in_change_and_management (archived at https://perma.cc/5D8N-Q8C7)

**7** Amazon Jobs, 29 October 2017, https://www.amazon.jobs/en/working/working-amazon (archived at https://perma.cc/T8YA-YLRQ)

**8** Satell, G (2017) *Mapping Innovation: A playbook for navigating a disruptive age*, McGraw-Hill, New York

**9** http://timkastelle.org/blog/2010/08/innovation-for-now-and-for-the-future/ (archived at https://perma.cc/GCK7-P5QX)

**10** Baghai, M, Coley, S and White, D (1999) *The Alchemy of Growth*, Perseus Books, New York

# Chapter 10

**1** https://hbr.org/2008/02/the-founders-dilemma (archived at https://perma.cc/6JBW-T8XX)

# Chapter 12

1  https://techcrunch.com/2017/05/17/heres-how-likely-your-startup-is-to-get-acquired-at-any-stage/ (archived at https://perma.cc/Y4LT-99PQ)

# Chapter 13

1  Herzberg, F, Mausner, B and Snyderman, BB (1959) *The Motivation to Work*, 2nd edn, John Wiley, New York

# Chapter 15

1  https://www.linkedin.com/pulse/biggest-change-my-business-life-carl-reader/ (archived at https://perma.cc/82R8-Q6QF)

# INDEX